Gulf Publishing Company
Book Division
Houston, Texas

AND NOW... THE NEWS

Mike Wolverton

To My Daughter Karelyn,
With Love & very special thanks &
joy!

Mike Wolverton

To Ruth
who insisted
because she had faith

Acknowledgments

I would like to thank all my friends and associates
from whom I have learned so much over the years.
Special thanks to Joe Beck, whose inspiration
sustained me through those crazy, hazy early days
of television. I am grateful to Liz Herbert for her
invaluable help with the manuscript, and to my
editor, Tim Calk, for his hard work and many worthwhile suggestions.

Contents

Preface

"Ladies and gentlemen, I am afraid my subject is rather an exciting one and as I don't like excitement, I shall approach it in a gentle, timid, roundabout way."

Max Beerbohm in a radio broadcast

To paraphrase, ladies and gentlemen, I am afraid my subject is quite an exciting one and as I thrive on excitement, I have approached it in an aggressive, brash, very direct way.

This has not always been so.

During much of my journalistic career I suffered from the objectivity syndrome. I had been carefully taught, and I therefore believed, that reporting should be objective—just the facts—nothing subjective—none of the feeling. But one day I asked myself, "What facts? Why are *facts of feelings* not important to communicate? I am a subjective being reporting to other subjective beings. Who do you think you are," I chided myself, "Mister Spock reporting to the Vulcans? Where are your pointed ears?"

Then I made a serious mistake.

As I tossed out the dirty bath water of objectivity, I carelessly lost the baby, responsibility. To assuage my loss I adopted a series of motley moppets such as advocacy journalism, checkbook journalism, jugular journalism, and, I blush to confess, that entertainer in journalistic clothing, tabloid journalism.

I finally retrieved my first born and true love, responsible journalism. I realized that the facts of any news story must include the facts of the emotional, or subjective, content of the story. Although my ears may now blush to passion pink, they are no longer garish green and pointed. I no longer infuse false emotions into my stories to make them seem exciting. If they are exciting, it is because of their own innate subjective content, which I have to dig out and communicate along with the so-called facts.

The innate subjective content of my subject here, the art and craft of responsibly reporting the news through the broadcast media, is that we, as journalists, must feel responsible for getting our fellow human beings safely into the twenty-first century. It is going to be our ability to communicate the full spectrum of the meaning of events during this final quarter of the twentieth century that will enable us and the constituents of our republic to survive. That survival depends upon a well-informed electorate. We have been handed the hardware to do the job. It is we, the software, that will be to blame if a new century's party is given on December 31, 1999, and nobody comes. We must use all of the new technology of this electronic news gathering age to teach, to illuminate, to empathize; yes, Virginia, even to inspire!

That is why I find my subject so exciting.

Writing about the art and craft of broadcast journalism and its responsibility has helped me immeasurably to get it all together for myself. If reading what I have written about the subject helps students preparing for a career in broadcast journalism, or serves as a mid-career reinforcer for working broadcast journalists, my excitement will be compounded tremendously.

I shall look forward to swirling a lemon peel and singing "Auld Lang Syne" with you at the new century's party as we toast the health of our intact republic and its informed constituents.

Mike Wolverton
Austin, Texas
July—1977

Part I

Everything you ever wanted to know about broadcast journalism but were afraid to ask.

1

What's the Use of Being Human?

Human beings have an amazingly limited repertoire of things to be experienced, not because our environment is such a wasteland, but because our culture dictates what experiences we must have and inhibits those we must not have. If our culture states that we are the "Pot Smokers of America," then we must experience pot smoking. We must not, under any circumstances, experience non-pot smoking lest we be labelled misfits.

Our so-called western culture in the late twentieth century does allow us to pick a role, any role. But once that role is picked we must play it out on a very tiny stage. If we pick the role of "leading-light-of-the-community," we must have only leading-light experiences. We must not have any "carefree-bum-on-the-roam" experiences. If we choose the carefree bum role, what crack do we get at leading-light experiences?

I'm not knocking it. This limited repertoire of experience is probably necessary to the maintenance of human culture. We are social animals and we die if we get to feeling lonely or "out of it." I am also not knocking it because it is this monotonous fabric of human experience that is the raw material from which we make our news stories. It isn't much, but it is all we've got.

How do we weave colorful, award-winning, rating-snatching news banners out of this gray cloth? Let me tell you about my friend, Harry Schneider. Harry is an artist. He bills himself as "The

Fastest Draw in the West." You can meet Harry at almost any big art show in southern Texas. You will recognize him by his enormous grin stated parenthetically between lush sideburns. He'll be wearing a Tyrolean hat and working intently at a portable easel. Pose for Harry for a few seconds and his charcoal moves over a large piece of drawing paper at sonic speed. In less than a minute Harry will produce an amazing likeness of you.

"How do you do it, Harry?" you ask.

"There's always one significant feature that makes you *you* and nobody else," Harry replies, "I find that characteristic and emphasize it. That'll be two dollars, please."

That parenthetical grin appears again. You pay Harry his two dollars and take your portrait home, but what you've really gotten is a million dollars worth of advice on how to make news out of human experience!

How do we become the Harry Schneiders of speaker and tube? We take an oath on our cassette recorders and cameras never to bounce back human experience like a Polaroid ten-second wonder—not even if we are in a hurry, which we usually are and not even if we are "new journalists" and think that this is what we are supposed to be doing. Would Harry be caught dead making quicky snapshots and dealing them back to his customers? No. Harry is an artist and a craftsperson. It is the artist in him that enables him to see that one significant characteristic in each and every human face. It is the craftsperson he has trained himself to be that enables him to use his tools and the techniques of his trade to emphasize that feature and to develop it into an interesting and valuable portrait.

We, too, must become artists and craftspersons. Artists enough to pick the one element from the sameness of the particular human experience we are reporting and concentrate our story on it. Then, as craftspersons, using the tools of our trade, we'll develop that characteristic, that unique feature, into an interesting and valuable news story, though we may have only a minute between the time we make our observation and the time we are on the air reporting it.

If we can do this, even in our quick draw reports, our fellow human scene watchers will recognize the uniqueness in the experience we relate. They will be delighted with the dash of living color we splash on the gray-to-gray background of their own experience. What's more, they will tell those recording angels, "I listen to *that* newsperson's reports!"

Ah, yes. Those recording angels.

All artists-craftspersons get feedback from the public and the critics one way or another. We get ours by the numbers. The angels who record these numbers go by many names—Neilson, ARB, Hooper—and they are everywhere. Someone, somewhere in each market area, samples broadcast listeners and watchers. They write down these numbers in the Great-Book-Believed-By-All, the favorite reading matter of advertising agencies' time buyers. Okay. If it's the numbers game they want to play (and it is), then it's the numbers game we play. Don't sweat it. We can play the numbers game and still survive as responsible broadcast journalists. What the numbers tell us is how good we are as craftspersons. Well-crafted news reports and programs are the ones that *do* get the ratings. So let's look at our numbers. If they are low, maybe we are not using our tools or applying our techniques properly. We may have good raw material, we may be reporting on the right human experiences, but are we crafting those experiences into good news stories?

Numbers, Recording Angels, and Craftsmanship

The lives and fortunes of all broadcasters are in the hands of fewer than two thousand families. That is all it takes to decide what all other families are doing. No one doubts the accuracy of surveys made on a few families to determine the listening and viewing habits of millions of families. The principle is simple. If you toss a coin one hundred times and get heads fifty times and tails fifty times, you don't have to toss it a million times to know that heads and tails will come out about even. In fact, the statistical law is that the more numbers involved the closer theory and practice come together.

By keeping track of the radio listening and TV viewing habits of some 1800 families, carefully selected to represent a proper social, political, and economic cross section, the habits of the entire nation can be accurately determined. This is how the numbers game is played. Neilson and Arbitron (ARB) folks are the largest and the ones most relied upon to bring the broadcaster his/her rating—his/her numbers. These numbers are obtained by electronic devices attached to the broadcast receivers of the sample families and/or by diaries kept by the families. The recording angels can even give you a demographic profile of your audience—telling you how many rich, how many poor, how many teenyboppers, or senior citizens are tuned in.

These numbers are worth pure gold. They are recorded weekly, monthly, or quarterly, in the Great Book consulted by advertisers and their time buyers. The higher your numbers the more money charged by your station or network for the commercial announcements run in your newscasts or adjacent to them.

Time buyers like to buy time on the basis of thousands of homes tuned in to your program. They often agree to pay for the client's spot announcements on the basis of one dollar per thousand homes. If your rating goes up one point and this number represents one million homes, it doesn't take much computing to figure out that your company has made a cool one thousand dollars on that one point rating increase. The other way around, of course, they can lose a thousand.

The numbers game puts Las Vegas to shame. But there is one difference—this is a game you can rig in your favor.

I have found that people instinctively recognize and are attracted to well-crafted news stories and newscasts. Perhaps because they are all made from human experience, or perhaps we all have a good feeling for craftsmanship whether its weaving, cabinetwork or storytelling. At any rate, human experience, well crafted into the news idiom, gets high numbers every time. There are no "good" news programs that remain in oblivion. People smell them out every time and the station or network that produces them gets a boost in their overall rating from the recording angels.

You can check this out for yourself by checking up on the radio and television stations that consistently have the top ratings in any ADI (area of dominant influence). Like a fever goes with the measles, this situation always pin-points a broadcast station with a strong news department staffed by excellent news craftspersons. In my consulting work I have invariably improved a station's overall ratings by helping the news department people become better craftspersons. Human beings know and seek out those of us who can manage to make something skillful of human experience.

That raw human experience is pretty drab, remember? It is about as drab as the potter's clay or the weaver's sheep's rump. But the potter doesn't hand you a fist full of his mud and tell you it is a pot, nor does the weaver hand you a sack of raw wool that is freshly clipped from a sheep and tell you it is a sweater! Similarly, we as broadcast journalists cannot throw raw human experience at our audience and call it the latest news. Raw human experience, like raw wool or clay, must be crafted into an artifact—*artifact news*.

Now, let's take some raw human experience to the shop and work it into a good, honest artifact worth presenting to the public as something called news.

The Balcones Heights Home Owner's Association is protesting a rezoning ordinance which will allow apartment complexes in their area. Association members say they object to the high population density that the new apartment complexes will bring to their neighborhood. Members say they especially fear the additional traffic problems that an increase in population density will create around their elementary school, which is already troubled by too much automobile traffic.

That's the story and it's a drab one. Just a very common, garden variety urban problem. How do we report it? Tell it like it is, just a few lines of copy read into microphone and camera? No. That would be like the potter pushing mud in your eyes. Let's pick out one element we want to characterize and hang our story on it.

Intuition is your guide to recognizing the particular characteristics which "make" a story. You can sharpen your intuition in this regard by studying political cartoons. The political cartoonist picks out one characteristic of a political leader and draws it boldly—the Nixon nose, the Carter teeth. Look at the individuals involved in your story. Is there one who is the catalyst? Look at the setting. Is it unique? Look at the characteristics of the conflict. Is there humor? Pathos? Look for unusual ironies and paradoxes. Among these individual elements of the story you will find at least one which seems to you to *characterize* the story. Zoom in on it and draw it large.

The Balcones Heights Home Owner's Association is motivated by concern for the safety of their children. They are fighting city hall, which is motivated by a special interest group. (A prominent citizen donated generously to the campaign fund of several of the city councilmen.) We have conflict and therefore drama. So we zero in on our protagonist, the leader of the Home Owner's Association, one human being who will catalyze the reaction from city hall. We focus our cameras and microphones on him and ask a leading question.

Reporter—Mr. Jim Garrett, do you honestly feel that these new apartment complexes in your neighborhood will endanger your children?

Garrett—Well, according to a survey we had made, traffic on the street in front of the school would be increased tenfold. The kids wouldn't be safe! When we bought our homes in this subdivision the sales people made a big thing out of the fact that it was zoned residential. We'd never have to worry, they said. But as soon as the big money interest wants to change things the city dads bow and scrape. Screw the people! I'll tell you though, we're going to fight this thing! We're going to fight for our kids and our neighborhood!

Again, just a few lines of copy, but *voiced* by the protagonist in a drama. What a difference.

One final thought about human experience as raw material for artifact news. The potter doesn't use any old clay as raw material, because an artist-craftsperson is particular about the qualities inherent in his material. In crafting broadcast news we also need to be concerned about the inherent qualities of the human experience we select as our raw material.

The raw material richest in potential for fashioning worthwhile and successful news artifacts will be social material that has been tempered by economics and hardfired in the kiln called politics. Social, economic, and political experience are the best clays we can mine from which to craft our daily offerings. It will be this body of human experience that we will sharpen and emphasize with the tools and techniques of our craft—the craft of broadcast journalism.

Man Bites Dog

There are no craft secrets in broadcast journalism. The key to success is how you project your personality, or more accurately perhaps, which facet of your personality you project for the purpose of reporting the story. This, in turn, will depend on whether you work within the frame of the "old" journalism or the "new" journalism.

In the old journalism the basic units of reporting are the data, the facts, the pieces of information. If we get the data on who, what, when, where, and why, we have our story. We then relate these facts in a so-called objective manner.

A Hottentot man has bitten an Eskimo dog at high noon on an ice floe in the Colorado River because, he said, "I wish to draw the attention of the news media to the injustices perpetrated by our society's dog-eat-dog attitude".

That's our lead. Then we dig for some background facts on the Hottentot man and the Eskimo dog. We would try to draw the man out on the injustices he mentioned, and we might even do an "in depth" study of ice floes in the Colorado River. We would, in all cases, work with pieces of information and join them together for our reports.

The facets of our personality projected while treating the story in this informational manner would flash before the public a sensitivity to discerning fact from fiction and a certain tenacity for "digging out the data." The whole story would grow out of our lead and would simply be an elaboration of the facts contained therein. Working in the frame of the old journalism our problem is to gather all the information. Then we have the "whole" story.

In the new journalism (not to be confused with advocacy journalism, a cop-out) the basic reporting unit is the *scene*. Our problem is to stay with the protagonist long enough for the scene to develop. We have a beginning to our report but it is not a lead. It might go something like this.

> The arrows of outrageous fortune have been suffered by Hottentot, Sam Jones, for as long as he can bear. Today, he bit the dog that bites him.

This is our "narrative hook." By now you may be saying, "Scene . . . protagonist . . . narrative hook—what are we writing, a short story?" You are right. We are writing what has been called a nonfiction short story! More accurately, it is a true story structured and told, or shown, in the form of a drama. We stick to the facts and make nothing up—we must not—but we present the story to our audience as human drama, which it is. We look for plot, mood, time, and place. We "make the scene" and stay with it and record and photograph until the scene plays out. Our story *unfolds*, and the ending is usually more important than the beginning.

The beginning, or hook, should do four things: (1) present the protagonist, (2) bring in his opponent, (3) establish a mood, and (4) "plant" the ending. The ending will contain a twist, surprise, or explain the gimmick, if any. It will give the audience an extra *something*. It may be a laugh, a shock, or tear in the eye, a lump in the throat—something to convey the emotional or subjective value that every human experience has, that every news story worth reporting has. This beginning and this ending must not be far apart! In between our protagonist is facing a crisis.

A story I did on the problem of a city park director and his beautification program was written in the nuevo journalistic style and was picked up by a national news service and by a regional network. It was written to be read in one minute and it was structured exactly like an O'Henry short story.

Jack Robinson, director of Austin's city parks, looks out over the banks of Town Lake at the gnawed stumps of recently planted cypress and willow trees, and despairs of his beautification program. He wishes, perhaps, that city beavers would stay on the backs of well-heeled citizens. This may be hard to believe, but the buck-toothed beaver has become Robinson's number one problem! Not as surprised as the rest of us, but with no solution to the problem is Pierce Uzell, a biologist with the Texas Parks Department. He simply says that beavers are more common than most people think, and that Bucky Beaver is alive and well in the shadow of downtown Austin. Robinson also tried wrapping the trees with chicken wire. But the beavers still chop the city's timber and carry it off to construct their dams and lodges. But there is one solution that has brought a gleam to the eyes of Park Director Robinson. It is, it turns out, quite legal to trap beavers in Travis County. Now. If there is someone who would like to go into the fur business . . . Robinson's beautification program will leap ahead. And the capitol city may have the first downtown fur trapping business in history!

The first ten seconds of the story, the narrative hook, presents the protagonist, brings in his opponent, establishes a mood, and plants the ending twist. We have placed our protagonist in a crisis. We show, or imply, during the next forty seconds, the struggle our hero has had to try to solve his problem. But alas! Neither an expert, nor the use of hardware can solve his problem. It seems hopeless. But in the last ten seconds a solution appears, like the cavalry charging across the horizon, and a surprise "twist" is frosted on.

Any news story, hard or soft, funny or sober, can be structured in this fashion. This kind of structure will transmit the feeling content of any human episode because of its dramatic impact. The techniques of story-form are designed to do just that.

The facet of our personality, then, which we project in treating the story as drama will flash before the public a sensitivity to feeling, and an ability to sequence the story in its most interesting aspect. When we have given our audience the *human value* of the scene, then we will have the "true" story.

Whether you work in the classical or the nuevo journalistic style depends on the personality you choose to project. Most of us find it easier to go after just the facts. The public's right to know has been widely discussed and is mostly accepted. One can ask questions about facts without too much personal embarrassment. But working to develop the dramatic aspects of the story often requires asking questions to which we have no right to expect answers, and asking to see things we are not entitled to see. It often leads to a personal involvement with the protagonist that can be emotionally draining and dangerous. The danger is that we get so close to our protagonist that we lose sight of our job as reporter and become instead a press secretary. We must be accustomed to being brazen at times and must never feel that we must protect our "hero"!

Try to remember what Harry Truman said, "If you can't stand the heat, stay out of the kitchen." There is always the cool veranda of the old journalism.

Whether our news story is crafted in the kitchen or out on the veranda, we must stand accountable for our behavior. We must be answerable to the way in which we have told our story. We must be *responsible* news broadcasters. Responsibility is the ethics of our craft. In a democracy the journalist is accountable to the people for the picture of reality he gives them. The consequences of irresponsibility are the weakening and, ultimately, the collapse of the free society. We cannot exist as a free society without a relevant picture of reality on which to base our decisions. This requires us to keep our maps and our territories straight. The map is *not* the territory!

Maps and Their Territories

General semantics is the most useful frame of reference we have for responsible news broadcasting. Now don't go running to your abridged or unabridged for a definition. Dictionaries are practically useless for finding out the definitions of words. Really! A dictionary is a great device for finding out an acceptable pronunciation for a word, and I recommend its constant use for this purpose. But if you wish to find out what a word actually means, forget *Webster's*. Stop and think for a moment. A dictionary defines words by using more words. Then you look up the words in the definition and find *those* defined by still more words. Mathematicians (who have a semantically pure symbol language) call this "infinite regression"— meaning it gets you nowhere. For example, you look up "marvelous" and find it means "stupendous." So you look up "stupendous" and guess what? You learn that it means "marvelous." Big deal.

Mathematicians and physicists have devised a way out of the dilemma. According to P.W. Bridgman, a physicist, "The true meaning of a term is to be found by observing what a man *does* with it, not by what he *says* about it." Bridgman, a Nobel prize winner, has shown us that the meaning of a word lies in the *operation*—the things done by and to it that establish its validity. For example, a physicist defines the word "electron" by showing us what an electron does, how it operates. Shoot it across a photographic emulsion in an electric field and it makes a black line which always curves to the positive side of the electric field. Other tests show that the electron has such and such a mass, spin, charge, etc. From observation an operational definition of "electron" is made. Physicists know what an electron is by what it *does*—not by what Mr. Webster or anybody else *says* about it. A physicist never says, "I hate all electrons," or, "Some of my best friends are electrons." Electrons are not good or bad, they are just electrons and they behave in certain predictable ways. Of course, electrons can do good or bad things. If you strap a man down in a wired-up chair and send a lot of electrons through his body and kill him, then that man could say electrons were doing a bad thing. However, the man's society might say the electrons were doing a good thing. As my grandfather used to say, "It all depends whose horse is getting whipped!"

The important lesson our semanticists have for us is that this operational definition of words can and should be applied outside the physical sciences where Dr. Bridgman originated it. In fact, we ought to use operational definitions exclusively as we go about our daily grind of news reporting.

For example, take M.T. Glass, news director of TV station KRAP, Broken Bottles, Mississippi. Let's look in on him back in 1955, before all the civil rights hassle started. He picks up an application for a job for his news department, and the first thing he sees is "Race: Negro." He drops the application into the waste basket. He might mumble something like, "The Broken Bottles community wouldn't cotton to any Negras in my news department." What the word "Negro" meant to Glass couldn't have been found in any dictionary, not even one compiled by a red-neck. It could only have been found in his operation on seeing the word, i.e., the *action* of dropping the black man's application in the waste basket without looking to see if the man was qualified. But operational definitions change with time. And time marches on. We look in on our same M.T. Glass, news director, in the early spring of 1972. Just as the magnolias are budding outside his window he again picks up an application for a job in his news department, and again the first thing he sees is "Race: Negro." Now he rushes over to the telephone and calls the man and offers him a job. "Gotta lotta blacks in my community," Glass might say to himself, "Gotta develop me a black news man." So you see what the word "Negro" means is not in the dictionary, or in the stars, but within ourselves and what we *do* in response to the word.

Alfred Korzybski, the educator and scientist who pioneered the science of general semantics, tells us we should not pay attention to words themselves but to the semantic reactions—the human responses to symbols, signs, and symbolic systems. That, of course, applies to the pictures we broadcast as well as the words we broadcast. Both are parts of our symbolic system of news broadcasting.

Pigs are *not* always pigs as the railroad agent in P.G. Woodhouse's famous story insisted they were, or as Wendel Johnson, author of *People in Quandaries: The Semantics of Personal Adjustment,* said, "To a mouse, cheese is cheese—that's why mouse traps work."

A responsible newsbroadcaster, then, must use words and pictures that portray the news in terms of the operational qualities of those words in his community at the time of the broadcast. And this is where maps and their territories enter into the picture. Semanticists are often derided because of their insistence that the map is not the territory—the *word* is not the *thing.* My first reaction, and probably yours also, was that this was perfectly obvious. Anybody would know that!

Hardly anybody knows that!

Just recently I covered a news story about a superintendent of a public school system who was campaigning to eliminate a certain plainspoken dictionary from all high school libraries. His reason was that this dictionary contained definitions of obscene words. He argued that students must be protected from such influences, because knowledge of evil (he considered knowledge of words having to do with forbidden sexual behavior as evil) would incite evil. This common conception that the mere knowledge of words can be the cause of behavior described by those words is a kind of word-magic. We are all susceptible to word-magic if we do not learn our lessons in semantics. This is an example of what the general semantics people mean when they say people often confuse words with things—the map with the territory.

If we meet a young lady who is introduced to us as a Ms. Tomokoto, we can hardly resist the impulse to ask her if she is Japanese even though she may have red hair and blue eyes and speak with an Irish brogue. She may be married to a Japanese, or she might have ancestors who came from Japan generations ago, or she might be of Slavic origin and her name might only be the result of dropping several extra consonants into the ocean on the way over. Don't take for granted that we really know that the word is not the thing. We're all brainwashed the other way around.

We must now practice reverse brainwashing by reminding ourselves that the symbol *is not* the thing symbolized; the map *is not* the territory; the word *is not* the thing. I recommend chanting those three statements for five minutes every day. I also recommend keeping a scrapbook of anecdotes, clippings, and quotes from broadcasters that illustrate the confusion of symbols and things symbolized. Look for examples of instances where people appear to think there is a necessary connection between words and what words stand for. My favorite is a quote from a woman who, on being told that an unmanned spacecraft used the star Arcturus as a navigational aid, remarked, "Isn't it wonderful how those astronauts know the names of all those stars." I also collect quotes that illustrate the lack of confusion between words and what they stand for. So far no one has topped Shakespeare's, "A rose by any other name would smell as sweet." After collecting many such samples I find it easy to recognize similar patterns of thought in my fellow broadcasters and in myself.

Much of today's irresponsible broadcasting is a result of confusion on this very basic principle of general semantics. We most offend when we insert the verb form "is" into our copy as in, "Detroit is a crime-ridden city." Detroit by any other name . . .

Another important lesson that general semantics teaches is there are *reports*, there are *inferences,* and there are *judgments*—and never the trio should meet. Semantics tell us there are no inferences in a report. There are no judgments in inferences (and no reporting, either). There is no report in a judgment, nor is there inference. Reports, inferences, and judgments all have their place, but they must never be mixed up together in a report.

A report is a report is a report.

If we wish to give information we must give a report. A report of what *we* have seen, heard, or felt. To make a report one must adhere to two rules: (1) your information must be *verifiable,* (2) it must *exclude* inferences and judgments.

"There are landing lights on each side of the runway," is a report. So is, "There are no apples left in the basket." You may also have a report of a report, for example, "The Nile is the longest river in the world . . . Rome fell in A.D. 476 . . . The *New York Times* says in a front page story that a prominent Russian diplomat was arrested for drunken driving." A report is something that can be verified. It does not imply anything, and it does not make any judgments.

The news, then, is not reported with respect to what people say, but with respect to what they do. It is the way in which they act that clues us in to the meaning of an episode of human experience and gives us the "handle" for a meaningful report.

Reporting is not repeating. Repeating an episode of human experience will never inform people about what is really going on. What is going on, or the *semantic value* of the episode, must be determined and then reported, and this report should not contain any inferences or judgments. Inferences and judgments will enter into the reporter's work, but they will come in the feature story, the documentary, and in other forms of broadcastable non-news. They will enter into what we report as news, hard or soft, only when we fail in our work as broadcast journalists.

2

So What's News?

Everyone has heard the old adage, "There's nothing new under the sun." Well, it's wrong. One day in July, in 1969, Neil Armstrong stepped out of his spaceship onto the surface of the moon. That had never happened before in the whole history of mankind. It was something new that was happening under the sun. It was, therefore, news—hard news—as hard as news can get because it was the biggest news story yet. What could mankind do for an encore? A manned landing on another planet in another galaxy will not top that news story because it will be *another* manned landing on *another* heavenly body. So, when the first astronaut sets his foot upon Mars it will be news, but softer news than the Neil Armstrong feat. Probably not until the first manned landing in future or past *time* will we have a suitable encore—a harder news story than the first moon landing.

"History repeats itself" is another old adage, and it's true. On July 4, 1975, Jennifer Stonewall Jackson died at the wheel of her Gremlin after crashing into a bridge railing following a brief seventy-mile-an-hour nap. She was the 423rd person to die in a traffic mishap that day in the U.S., the 4,624th that year, and 230 millionth since Marcus Claudius Nero dozed at the reins of his speeding chariot, hooked a wheel on a bridge abutment and looped-the-loop into the Tiber river, drowning forthwith. What happened to Jennifer and Marcus has happened over and over again in the history of mankind. It was history repeating itself; repeating itself with such predictable regularity that it was hardly news at all. It was personal tragedy for Jennifer, perhaps, and for her family and friends, certainly, but it was not news. Between the commonality of the Jennifer Jackson tragedy and the uniqueness of the Neil Armstrong triumph, lies a continuum of news—a "hardness scale"—along which news is news is news according to the frequency with which such things happen under *our* particular sun.

This scale is, of course, only a scale and must be calibrated to measure something before it becomes a tool for the news broadcaster. It must therefore be laid against an area of interest before one has an assessment of the news value of a particular happening. There is a whole county in West Texas in which no fatal automobile accident has ever occurred. Now, if Jennifer had been a resident of this county and had died there, and you were reporting news only to residents of that county, it would measure out as a very hard news story. It would be a first time, not-very-probable happening. By the same measure if we are reporting the news to our entire galaxy and Neil Armstrong was the eleven millionth space voyager to have made the milk run from his home planet to one of the planet's moons, the news value would be so soft you could stir it with a straw. "So what else is new?" said the Galaxian as he shoved off into a time warp for the tenth time that week.

So news, then, is something that is truly new that has not happened within the knowledge and history of the audience to whom you are reporting.

Back in the days when we were all quite provincial, certain rules could be made about local, regional, national, and international news. It was thought that local news was of first rank interest to the local populace and the farther away from the province a happening occurred the less likely were the people to be interested in this news. That, of course, was before a quiet meeting of sheiks in far-off Arabia put your friendly neighborhood filling station out of business.

In spite of the fact that our province has expanded to "Village Earth" and thereby changed what is news to our local market audience, we still tend to pay more attention to the wreck on the highway than to the latest meeting of the Gnomes of Zurich. We tend to overlook the fact that when the Gnomes agree on a new price for gold, the value of the Yankee dollar comes down a peg or two and thereby reduces the value of our paycheck by at least three wieners.

We fall into this trap because we tend to think about what news is in terms of what we imagine our listeners, or viewers, are interested in. We think Tireless Joe Hubcap, who owns the corner filling station and watches the news out of the corner of his eye, is going to be more interested in the convenience store robbery down the street than in what the Arabs are up to in the Middle East. And so he will. But that is only because Tireless Joe H. has not made the connection between the Arab Oil Consortium and butter he puts on his family's table. If he *knows* that what the Arabs are deciding has a direct effect on whether or not he will be in business next year, you can bet your bottom tape cassette that he is going to listen to the news broadcast that can tell him what the Arabs did today and could care less about the robbery or the latest wreck on the highway. The rub is that unless we, as responsible broadcast journalists, *make the connection* for our audience, they will not know what news they should be most interested in.

Now we come face to face with the greatest difficulty of our profession. What, exactly, is our mission as we go about our job of selecting and reporting what is the news? Journalists are a vital part of the central communications system for a people struggling to remain free and stable in a little blue spaceship called Earth. Because of our deadlines, we are under almost constant "red alert," admonished to man our battle stations. What battle stations? Where? What *are* we supposed to be doing? It is difficult for us to be clear about our mission. When we try to explain it to ourselves and to others, it most often comes out in meaningless clichés. Like Editor Walter Burns says in *Front Page,* "Print the news and raise hell!" or, in the more dignified version of Joseph Pulitzer, "Afflict the comfortable and comfort the afflicted!"

One of our own broadcast journalists, Fred W. Friendly, has put our mission into words better than most. Friendly defines what a journalist does this way, " . . . an explainer of complicated issues," and he says, " . . . If you can't understand them, you can't explain them."

In his remarks prepared for delivery at the dedication of the School of Communication Complex at the University of Texas at Austin on March 14, 1975, Friendly said, "What makes the modern day journalist essential is his or her ability to explain . . . his or her skill in print or broadcast communications to provide a picture of reality on which members of society can act."

In 1922, the year commercial radio broadcasting was born, Walter Lippmann wrote in *Public Opinion,* "The press . . . is like the beam of a searchlight that moves restlessly about, bringing one episode and then another out of the darkness into vision." The searchlight is the light of understanding. We must focus the light of understanding on those episodes we pick out and report on and call the news.

What it all boils down to is that our mission is to understand. If *we* understand, then we will know that the meeting of a little band of Arab sheiks is the *local* news today. And if we *understand,* we will come on the air with the news that "A meeting in Saudi Arabia today may make the neighborhood American filling station as obsolete as a railroad lantern." *That* lead will get the attention of Tireless Joe H. and will provide him with a picture of reality on which he can act.

Like the early bird that thought he had caught two worms only to discover he had the head and tail of the same worm, the journalist must remember that everything is connected to everything else. The head of the worm may be the weather in Brazil, but the tail is that fifty-cent cup of coffee at Ye Friendly Neighborhood Coffee Shoppe in Upper Ypsilanti, Michigan.

In order to understand the meaning of the new things that happen here in our little corner of the Milky Way, the broadcast journalist must be curious about everything and try to imagine how it all might fit together; a constant learner; a collector of disparate information; a generalist who spends this lifetime in the pursuit of a little knowledge about a lot of things.

As we move restlessly about, viewing and learning about one episode of human experience after another, we must ask, "What does it mean?" And in an age of specialization it is not always obvious what these episodes we will call news really do mean. But our mission is to find out, to go to the specialists if necessary and to get it all together so that we will understand and so that our audience will know.

What Tireless Joe H. didn't know cost him his business. Had we not finally come to know what Watergate *meant*, it would have cost us our democracy and our freedom. What we didn't know about the Tonkin Gulf, the energy crisis, and DDT damn near killed us all.

What do you and your community know about DNA recombinant research? Will it kill us or cure us, or will it lead scientists to their El Dorado where the genetic Rosetta stone is written in plain English? No matter how they slice their deoxyribonucleic acid, it is going to be a political hot potato for years. What do you know about the security precautions in Argentina's nuclear power plants? What's to prevent a terrorist group from heisting a little plutonium, tinkering together a Hiroshima-sized bomb and planting it at your home town airport? Have you understood and explained the mind-numbing complexity of nuclear proliferation on your "local" news lately? Time is running out if you expect to get yourself and your community into the twenty-first century alive and well.

It is not too much to say that the journalist, now in this final quarter of the twentieth century, will determine the survival of our civilization as we know it. What Edward R. Murrow said about television is true of the entire discipline of broadcast journalism.

> This instrument can teach; it can illuminate, yes and it can inspire. But it can do so only to the extent that humans are determined to use it to those ends. Otherwise it is merely lights and wires in a box.

3

So What Else Is News?

The "lights and the wires in the box" are responsive to much that is non-news, but this non-news is still the responsibility of the news broadcaster to produce. Paradoxically, it is from writing and producing broadcastable non-news the responsible reporter of human experience learns the most about his mission. Because of the thought and research required the area of the feature story, the documentary, the editorial, and the exposé, teaches us what the news means and offers us our greatest opportunity to explain that meaning. Because we are less shackled than usual by semantic considerations in the area of broadcastable non-news, inferences and judgments are admissible as conclusionary elements in our package of reportage.

Those of us working at the grass roots of broadcast journalism have found the most effective center of gravity for the meaning of the news to be city hall. From this center spin off miles and miles of audio and video tape non-news dealing with town planning, public health, child welfare, educational progress, inter-racial understanding, the hunt for more and cheaper energy, and ecology planning.

If democracy is to survive, and if it is really to be made to work for another two hundred years, it will be because we made it work at the grass roots level—down at city hall. You see, if I can feed my neighbors out of my home garden, then my country can feed the world out of its bread basket.

Is There a Documentary in the House?

It is a sad commentary on the state of grass roots journalism that the FCC ruling returning an hour of prime time to local TV stations resulted in not much more than a trickle of local documentary production. Our great opportunity to explain, to provide a picture of reality on which our local citizens can act to help their kids and themselves, got drowned in a sea of reruns and "B" movies.

And where is the FM radio station that puts its stereophonic and quadraphonic sound facilities for even one hour a week to the task of moving restlessly about its city's neighborhoods, bringing one episode and then another out of silence into multidimensional hearing? The drama-impact potential of stereo and quad sound is mind-boggling—at least to some of us old timers who remember the power and the glory of mono-radio documentaries such as the Ed Murrow series, *Hear It Now,* in the late forties.

This great opportunity, now going down for the third time, is a loss even to broadcasters interested only in the numbers game. The potential audience for documentary presentations that enlighten the local citizenry is tremendous. For example, Austin, Texas, a city of about one-half million, has more than fifty neighborhood groups banded together as viable political entities, ready to assault city hall to ensure the survival and livability of their little state room on spaceship Earth. They are *interested*. They will watch and they will listen. The time to produce regularly scheduled documentaries is now. In this final quarter of the twentieth century, effective grass roots broadcast journalism will pull more numbers than the best network situation comedy show. The "mini-cam and super sound" technology is available to bring this seemingly dead opportunity back to life. What we need are some skills on the part of our grass roots broadcast journalists. Those skills can be learned. Shall we give it a try?

Okay. Let's get back to the center of gravity—city hall. The life blood of any feature story, documentary, exposé or editorial comment is research.

> **re·search** (ri-surch′, re′ surch) *n* 1. careful, systematic, patient study and investigation in some field of knowledge, undertaken to establish facts or principles.

With that definition of research in mind, head for city hall with a notebook in hand. On your way down, pick a theme—any theme.

Just be sure you can state it precisely in twenty-five words or less. Sit down in the city hall pressroom and think about it. A good theme is one that is tied to some human need. Better still, it might be a theme associated with a *basic human drive*—like hunger. Why not hunger? How many hungry people are there right here in any city? How many are dying of malnutrition or malnutrition related diseases? How much of a problem is hunger in a city, *really*? How about the retired and the old people—the fixed income crowd—do they have enough money left for groceries after they pay their light bills? How about all those people out of work? What's the unemployment rate multiplied by the work force? How do those thousands of families manage to eat? Does anybody at city hall *know*? If they know, do they *care*? If they care are they *doing anything* about this profound human need?

Now, here is a theme in considerably less than twenty-five words: How City Hall Answers the Cry of Hunger in River City. Divide this topic into four or five major sections, writing Roman numerals I through IV or V in the notebook with four or five lines between. Those four or five lines, numbered with Arabic numerals, will become the sixteen to twenty-five sequences, running two to three minutes each, from which we will edit our finished presentation. This will cut to about one hour with time for commercial clusters.

We might come up with something that looks like this:

I Who is hungry?
1. East side, west side, all around the town—locate the pockets of hunger.
2. Institutional hunger: nursing homes, do they starve their clients?
3. Drug related starvation: heroin & alcohol . . .
4. Malnutrition among the affluent.
II Why are they hungry?
1. The "classical" poor—"Lo, they are with you always."
2. Does unemployment lead to hunger?
3. Relationship between mental health and hunger.
4. Children starving from abuse and neglect.
III What are they doing to solve their hunger problem? How do they cope?
1. Going to "welfare" for help.
2. Pensioners and others on fixed income—How do they budget for food?
3. How does your community garden grow?

4. Politics aside, how do food stamps and/or other federal food programs really work?

IV The answer from city hall
   1. How much responsibility does the city actually take for its hungry people?
   2. Council persons—How aware of the problem? What solutions do they suggest?
   3. City administrators—How aware? What plans and programs are planned or operating?
   4. The mayor answers the cry of hunger . . .

It is now obvious that there are no questions to be asked around city hall *yet*. There may be some telephone calls we can make right away from the pressroom. You can let your fingers do the walking for a little while to develop some leads. But soon there will be no choice but to apply shoe leather to concrete in the time-honored manner of the police and journalist investigator. When we understand what the cry is all about, we will then come back to city hall and see how they answer.

Set aside sixteen pages in the notebook, for each of the sixteen episodes to be taped. At the top of each page write in the heading used in the outline. After your investigations you will fill this page with a synopsis of the episode you will later put on tape. A loose-leaf notebook is a good idea for recording the results of your research, since the pages can be rearranged into the most efficient sequence for taping sessions, and then rearranged once more for final editing. Consult your one-page synopsis before each taping session, then play it by ear during the actual taping. This will encourage spontaneity within each episode, while ensuring unity in the final production.

When editing a documentary, exposé, feature story, or editorial, keep in mind that the theme of the production should be apparent within the first two or three episodes and the problem sufficiently advanced for the audience to anticipate plenty of action and conflict. The very first sequence should contain something important and unanswered to "hook" the audience before the first commercial cluster. Why is the wife of a well-heeled lawyer from the plush side of town being treated for malnutrition? Why did this emaciated five-year-old child nearly die of starvation when the rest of her family was well fed? Monologues and extended explanations should be left out of the first sequences. Wait for this until you have your audience thoroughly addicted to your subject matter.

Don't set out to make a villian or a hero out of the city or other government entity. There will be a hero and a villain, but let them develop in the minds and hearts of the audience. You are presenting facts and principles uncovered by research. Check and double-check your facts. Test and retest your principles. (By principles I mean basic assumptions such as, all humans are entitled to dignity and enough to eat.) Present point and counterpoint. Give everybody enough rope to either swing or hang—but let *them* do it! You do not have to solve the social, economic, or political problem you have uncovered. But you can catalyze the solution. There will be those in your audience ready and able to jump on the mayor, or the council person, or the institution with bouquets or bricks, or organized protest. You will have done your job if you have provided a picture of reality on which members of your society can act. Thus, broadcastable non-news often becomes news when a community group or individual springs into action. Thus, too, does news beget news, with the documentary serving as both father and midwife to new generations of community action. And community action is news.

"So Okay, But What's Your Opinion"

While the documentary, the exposé, and the feature story can be handled along the lines suggested in the hunger story, the editorial is often a different pot of porridge. It is shorter, to the point, and opinionated. It also often carries one into the tangled wildwood of the Fairness Doctrine, born twin to the broadcast editorial in 1949. The Fairness Doctrine was aimed at preventing broadcasters from becoming propagandists. It does this, but through a glass darkened by years of ambiguous interpretations. In spite of this never-never land created by the F.C.C., a March 1976 poll by *Editorial Magazine* found that only five percent of the broadcast stations regularly running editorials had plans to discontinue them. The same poll showed that sixty percent of the stations not then running editorials had plans to do so. The tide is coming in.

There are two safe and easy ways to swim in the editorial broadcast surf. One, use canned editorials. They are a time-honored tradition among newspapers and there are many sources for these gems of the generality. Most of these editorials are, of course, handed out by vested interest. You simply pick the vested interest of your choice, pop-a-top, and add voice. The other way is to go soft and attack the safe issues vigorously. Come out fighting for greener grass, mother love, bicycle safety, and milk for kids. But, if you are inclined to try a plunge into the turbulent waters of real contoversy, come on in, it's fine! However, there is the undertow, and to keep from being dragged out to sea, here are some tips from one who has on occasion found himself beyond the breakers.

Give yourself *time* to write a good editorial. Editorial deadlines are the most relaxed in the broadcasting business, so the time is available. Keep in mind that your editorial is a display window for your station. It should be the best piece of broadcasting your station does—the best writing and production that *you* ever do. Your audience will not necessarily accept what you have to say. No matter what the subject of the editorial there will always be critics waiting to swarm all over you. For example, there is the "constant replier," whose name you will find with great frequency in the Letters To The Editor column of your local newspaper. He is the professional expert-on-every-subject who always demands time to reply to your editorial. So your editorial must be deftly done and as palatable as possible. The first thing these critics and repliers will attack is a chink in your logic. So plug the holes.

The True-Blue Syllogism

It is difficult to find flaws in one's own logic. I suggest use of the professional logician's tool—the syllogism—to check your case, pro or con. A syllogism is a form of reasoning in which two premises are made and a logical conclusion drawn from them. When you have finished writing your editorial you must be able to reduce your argument to these three simple statements: a major premise, a minor premise, and a conclusion. For example:

Major Premise: All eggs have yolks.
Minor Premise: The object I hold in my hand is an egg.
Conclusion: Though I cannot see it and though I have not yet broken the egg, I must be in possession of a yolk.

To keep the egg off your face, the major premise must be true, preferably a rule that is generally accepted. The minor premise must also be true and is usually a special case of the general rule stated in the major premise. The conclusion must relate the major and minor premises by applying the special case to the general case. And there must be no shifting of terms in the conclusion.

In most cases you will need to make a persuasive case for the major premise. Who says *all* eggs have yolks? Do fish eggs? How do we know this? Perhaps many people have never broken a peacock egg. Cover all the bases. Show that your major premise is a general rule, universally accepted, and clearly define the exceptions.

Now you must muster evidence to support the minor premise. The evidence must leave no doubt that the object I hold in my hand is indeed an egg, and one that does not come under the exceptions established by the major premise.

Finally, state your conclusions in terms defined in the major premise and proven in the minor premise.

By extracting the core of your argument into the form of a syllogism you can make sure that your argument will hold together, because your logic is flawless and your strategy is true.

I generally do this after I have written the first draft. Then, if necessary, I strengthen my premises and make certain that they lead to the conclusion I have drawn and that I have not shifted terms. You may need to rewrite at this time or even start all over again. Keep at it until what you have written can be reduced to a syllogism that expresses the essence of your argument.

Now check what you have written for any waves of angry verbiage that may drown your audience and leave them unconvinced. Delete words, phrases, even whole paragraphs in order to trim the rhetoric and keep it lean. Stick to your evidence and logic if you want to persuade your audience that your opinion is right.

On the other hand, don't cut the guts out of your editorial either. Don't try to be "objective," or detached. Make sure your convictions can be detected by even the most casual viewer-listener. To paraphrase the historian, G.K. Chesterton, "The angry journalist sees one side of the question. The calm journalist sees nothing at all, not even the question itself."

"You Called Me a What?"

The worst current of all, one that can sweep you under while opinion surfing, is that swift current the propagandist makes when an issue must be obscured—the irrelevant personal attack. Attacking a person instead of an issue, or along with an issue, when it is the issue you are arguing, will get you nothing but trouble. The personal slur gets the attention of the audience every time and the issue gets obscured or even forgotten. If you must make a personal attack—and there will be times when you must—don't try to handle it in the same editorial. Guilt by association is no guilt at all. Personal attack editorials must be based firmly on provable facts. Remember that while commentaries and analysis segments of bona fide news programs are exempt from the personal attack rule, under the Fairness Doctrine, editorials are not. And though the truth is your defense in libel and slander suits, the truth cuts no Fairness Doctrine mustard with the F.C.C. You must notify any person or group you have attacked within a week of the broadcast, preferably in writing, and get a receipt that the notification was received. You must tell the person, or group, the date and time of the personal attack and identify the broadcast on which it was made. You must also, within one week, send the person or group a script or tape of what was said. Then you must offer the person or group a chance to come on the air and answer that attack. There are no exceptions, regardless of the truth of your attack.

One final word on editorial writing. Don't write it just to be read, write it to be produced. Use news footage if it's to be aired on TV, and actuality inserts and production sounds if it is airing on a radio station. Your editorials may be short, fat, and opinionated, but in all other aspects they must be well-crafted broadcast productions—the very best you can write and produce.

The Nature of Community Reality

The local radio or TV station can do a great deal in this whole area of broadcastable non-news. Each broadcast journalist has the obligation to justify his/her existence by calling attention to the various issues faced by his/her community and dealing with them in a manner that will enable the community to make rational decisions on the basis of some positive beliefs.

It is the positive beliefs held in the collective imagination of the community that creates and sustains the reality faced by the community. Belief spawns reality, it is not the other way around. If a community is crime ridden, it is because the members of the community have visions of crime dancing in their heads. And until these visions in the collective imagination are changed, no amount of money spent on crime prevention is going to change the community reality. What reporting the crimes does is to keep the vision alive and well in the minds of the individuals in the community, thus perpetuating the crime.

The journalist has direct access to the collective mind of his community and can influence the visions that dance in the heads of its members. The power of positive imagination to create and sustain reality has not yet been proven by science, but it is de facto wisdom to any thoughtful journalist. And even the scientists are nipping at our heels on this one. They were tipped off by something that did not take place on the streets of New York City on June 4, 1968. No one who lost a wallet in New York on that date got it back. That was unusual because it had already been established that forty-five percent of the people who lose their wallets on New York streets do have them returned. This figure was arrived at by a group of psychology students at the Columbia University Teachers College. Over a period of time they had dropped wallets on the streets and waited for them to be returned. Consistently, forty-five percent of the wallets were returned except on that one day, June 4.

On June 3, 1968, Sirhan Sirhan shot Robert F. Kennedy.

The researchers wondered if the news of Kennedy's murder had anything to do with whatever social bonds cause people to return wallets.

This started two social scientists, Stephen Holloway and Harvey Hornstein, on a line of research that would attempt to discover how various types of news media reports might affect social behavior. After ten years of research that has been duplicated by many other social scientists they came to some newsworthy conclusions. Among them, one conclusion hits us where we live. It seems that news about the evil deeds of others breaks social bonds. This disruption of group ties leads to antisocial attitudes and behavior.

You can fool your friends and neighbors if you wish into thinking that all you do is to report what is happening in your community, but don't buy that rationale for yourself. We must all realize that what we select to report is going into that collective community consciousness from whence comes what is happening in the community.

Naturally, we do have to report and get it right. We have to report the good, the bad, the ugly, and the beautiful. That's the news, but the broadcastable non-news can be anything we choose. And this is where we can begin to generate the kind of news we will be reporting in the future. This is where we can relate happenings aimed at enabling our friends and neighbors to form some positive beliefs.

What can the local radio and TV station actually do? If you are part of a high-crime community, seek out the do-gooders and build your documentaries around man's humanity to man in your community. There is some of it going on even in the worst of communities. Try to rebuild some of those social bonds you broke down on your regular news reports on the latest violence. Do you have a dream for your community? What kind of world would you *like* to live in? Talk to your community leaders. Do they have some positive beliefs that ought to be communicated to the rest of the community?

Even though I have never been in your community I can tell you that someone in your community is doing some sensible ecological planning; that someone is saving a bundle on utility bills by making use of the wind and the sun as cheap energy sources; that some teacher in some school in your community is doing an outstanding job of educating kids; that there is brotherly love going on somewhere in that community of yours; that you have a public health hero hiding out somewhere; and, yes Virginia, that there is a Santa Claus who fed some of those hungry people. All of these are prime subjects for your local documentary.

All non-news broadcast presentations should be designed to relate community happenings to the audience in a manner that will enable the audience to form some positive belief. They should be interesting and impelling, even entertaining—*but never entertainment*. The haunting spector of news broadcasts conceived and presented as entertainment programs is frightening.

Part II

*The rite of exorcism and
other readiness rituals.*

4

The Ghost in the Castle

One sure way to rattle the chains that bind a democratic society and drag that society into the cellars of dusty death is to program news for its entertainment value. Yet the spector continues to walk among us, chortling behind the mask of comedy with the "Ho Ho" boys on the television news team, or from behind the mask of tragedy, spurring on the cowboy mentality that keeps some folks glued to the police monitor in the radio news room:

Good afternoon Mr. and Mrs. Citizen and all the cars that make our drive time traffic jams, let's go to press! . . . Lock your doors and bar your windows! Two pretty and innocent housewives were savagely raped in their very own kitchens earlier this afternoon . . . Thirty-one people have died in mangled agony on the streets and highways of Big City this past week . . . The blood flowed knee deep in Duffy's Tavern last night while the barmaids were busy filling the gut buckets . . . In other news today Police Chief Catchem Quick told the Rotary Club at their noon luncheon that if the crime rate keeps climbing at the present rate, citizens may have to surrender their freedom to the nation's authorities in order to survive at all . . . And remember, KMAD News never sleeps!

Okay, I confess. That was a transcript of one of my nightmares and any similarity to any real radio news broadcast is purely coincidental. I have borrowed a trick from our physicists and presented a limiting case. Physicists say that the best way to determine the truth of a hypothesis is to consider that hypothesis operating at its most extreme outer limit, i.e., consider the limiting case. If the hypothesis becomes absurd at its limits then it likely is a bad hypothesis. If it still looks good in the limiting case then it is likely true.

The hypothesis that news broadcasts ought to be scary entertainment breaks down in the limiting case under the mask of tragedy. News by the "Happy News Team" on TV is no less ludicrous when taken to the limiting case under the mask of comedy:

Video	Audio
Fade in—Long shot news set as anchorperson, meteorologist, and sportsperson roll player piano on set.	**Booth Announcer:** From around the world by satellite relay—live and in living color—Channel 23 World Witness News! *(Teletype with laughter in background. Bring up laughter to drown out teletype. Barroom style piano accompaniment as news team sings to the tune of "Those Were the Days.")*
Truck in to medium three shot as they gather around the piano and mug it up.	
	All: Tonight the news will really swing, And without a tragic sting, Witness News don't miss a thing, These are the days!
Close-up: Anchorperson	**Anchorperson:** Congress wants to ration gas . . .
Close-up: Sportsperson	**Sportsperson:** Staubach threw a pretty pass . . .
Close-up: Meteorologist	**Meteorologist:** And looking in the weather-glass . . .
Medium three shot—Follow shot as anchorperson goes to news desk.	**All:** These are the days!
	Anchorperson: Hi there. Ho Ho Bo Ho here. Now for what's happening in that big wide wonderful world out there. *(Sits behind news desk on whoopee cushion. Whoopee cushion followed by off-camera raucous laughter by crew.)*

Anchorperson: *(Pulls cushion out from under self and tosses it aside)* Whata ya know, Witness news has just found the lost chord! (Picks up news copy) Congress today passed the most stringent gas rationing bill since World War II as the energy crisis worsens and the lights brown out from coast to coast. But World Witness News knows there is a silver lining. Reporter Cindy Brass has that story.

Video Tape:
Brass-Potter Interview

Cindy: We are sitting with Mr. Peeper Potter in his dimly lighted living room in beautiful old Suburbburg. Mr. Peeper, you seem a jolly old man for having lived long enough to remember gas rationing during World War II.

Peeper: Yes, well, I grow my own bean sprouts you see. I still have my own victory garden.

Cindy: The new gas rationing bill doesn't upset you, then?

Peeper: Oh, no, quite the contrary. I'm looking forward to it!

Cindy: Would you mind telling World Witness News why you are so happy about gas rationing?

Peeper: Yes. Well, during World War II you know, we had this kind of gas rationing and suddenly we all had to stay home. My wife and I finally got acquainted with each other!

Cindy: Thank you, Mr. Peeper Potter. From Old Suburbberg, I'm Cindy Brass, Channel 23 World Witness News!

Studio: Medium shot
anchorperson

Anchorperson: And now, TV's happiest meteorologist—Chalk Talk Charlie—who always wears a smile for *his* umbrella. Charlie, when is this rain gonna stop?

34

Meteorologist standing in front of weather map showing huge frontal system moving in on Big Town.	**Meteorologist:** Well, actually, Bo, we haven't had all that much rain. Thirty-nine inches in thirty-nine days. That's only just one inch per day!
Medium two shot anchorperson and sportsperson	**Sportsperson:** Fantastic! The Big Town Cowpokes will certainly be glad to know that they can now take off their hip-boots and return to cleated shoes!
	Anchorperson: The nation's most ad-<u>mired</u> team since the rains started *(groans all around)*
Cut to close-up of anchorperson	**Anchorperson:** Ain't we got fun! Now, for the Channel 23 World Witness newsreel—We were there when . . .

Okay. Now I have another confession to make. I have seen nearly every gag in that script on TV news programs while reviewing tapes of newscasts from around the country! The news presented from behind the mask of comedy is even scarier than what goes on behind the mask of tragedy. It is no longer news but only poor entertainment of the type described so well by Shakespeare as, " . . . a tale told by an idiot . . . signifying nothing!"

To quote a more modern comment on the subject we can turn to Richard Salant. As head of CBS news at the time ABC bought Barbara Walters at a celebrity price tag of five million dollars, he raised questions about the distinction between news business and show business. Salant commented, "I'm really depressed as hell. This isn't journalism—this is a minstrel show. Is Barbara a journalist or is she Cher?"

That is the question all of us in broadcast news have to answer for ourselves. Are we journalists or are we minstrels? Or are we some combination of the two? If we are honest I think we will have to admit that we are all some combination of the two.

To put the question in historical perspective we might look back to the days of Walter Winchell, when broadcast news was done by name people who got a lot of money, and when there was little journalism in it. Walter Winchell, most would agree, was about five percent journalist and ninety-five percent minstrel. In more recent times, especially while reporting on the exploration of space, I think most of us would agree that Walter Cronkite was about ninety-five percent journalist and only about five percent minstrel. I believe all of us will find ourselves somewhere in between.

What we have to keep in mind is that our programmers and our station operators are in the minstrel show business. This puts the center of gravity of broadcasting in the field of entertainment. We can expect to be constantly pulled toward the Winchell end of the scale. Especially when our ratings falter. But in broadcast news we get our ratings by employing better journalistic craftsmanship. We must therefore always make a conscious effort to move toward the Cronkite-reporting-on-space end of the scale by adding to the depth of the journalism we employ.

The public has both a *need* to be entertained and a *right* to know. It is because of their right to be informed that they tune us in, not because of their need for entertainment. If the broadcast news makes any contribution to entertainment it is to increase the need of the public to escape from the depth of the implications of the information we give them! But the minstrel show must follow the news broadcast—not be a part of it and only after a decent pause for station identification!

The problem of "blood and guts" journalism and the sister problem of minstrel show journalism is solved when those of us responsible for broadcasting the news realize that we have no mission to entertain and no calling to report constantly recurring personal tragedies. If we will then add to the depth of our journalist efforts by ferreting out stories about that which is really new, that which touches, or likely will touch all our lives, most of our problems of discretion will be solved. For example, if we simply do not report traffic and other "routine" fatalities, the discretionary problem of whether or not to use names before next-of-kin have been notified simply evaporates. If we are no longer concerned that our news has any entertainment value, we find that we no longer have very many discretionary problems. A case in point—rape stories. Rape is a personal tragedy for all concerned, but it is not news. Presented as news it is only a ghoulish attempt to entertain.

We must all work to exorcise the spector of entertainment from our broadcast news. All we do is add journalism.

5

Just Add Water and Wait for Godot

The history of the universe, the history of the world, and the history of your own community is a developing story. Today's news presents the latest developments in that ongoing epic. News grows out of history and current events. Few, if any, news stories break out of the blue. Nearly all news stories can be anticipated. You do not have to be psychic to be able to predict news events, or even write news stories before they happen—but it helps. The well-known newsman's hunch, however, is a normal function of the human mind with its precognitive machinery in gear.

Hunches can be developed both qualitatively and quantitatively. The trick is simple. Pay attention to them and follow through. The more often you do this the more frequently these hunches come and the more accurate the information you get through your hunches. The more any faculty is exercised, the stronger and more useful it becomes.

As far as reading the future is concerned, it appears that all probable events that can branch out from a present event are somehow warped into the matrix of time-space. The farther into the future an event is, the more difficult it is to predict because of the greater number of branching probabilities. The closer an event is, the fewer the probabilities and so the easier it is to get an accurate prediction. From the newsperson's frame of reference, if one gambles on the most probable event, the gamble will usually pay off with a very high batting average on hunches. The work of precognition can all be done with the conscious mind.

One of the most unexpected of news events in recent history was the assassination of U.S. President John F. Kennedy. It will serve to illustrate how I had every opportunity to anticipate the event. I did not anticipate Kennedy's assassination in spite of all the handwriting on the wall recorded by my own hand in a personal journal I was writing at the time. Persons referred to include my wife, Ruth, and children, Pete, Sylvia, and Melissa.

November 10, 1963—Ruth has just shown me an article in the December issue of *Redbook* magazine which came today. It is written by Jhan Robbins and reports on a survey made in Europe to find out what children, aged five to nine, think Americans are like. The first paragraph, out of the mouth of a European babe, reads, "The average American is, of course, a Texan. He eats lots of breakfast and gets fat so he has to go on a diet because he likes to look skinny. He calls everyone 'sweetheart' and is bad to colored people. If he doesn't like who is president he usually shoots him."

Ruth thought this bit was not funny—"one of the 'hate Kennedy' Texans just might try to shoot him when he comes to Dallas," she said. I told her not to get hysterical. The specter of a presidential assassination in Dallas is pretty farfetched. But a Stevenson-type stoning could occur. (Adlai Stevenson, then U.S. Ambassador to the United Nations, had actually been stoned a few weeks earlier when he had tried to make a speech in Dallas.) The hate campaign is getting organized for the presidential visit to Dallas. It shapes up as a heckling campaign which flies the banner of "Free Speech." The American Fact Finding Committee seems to be arranging the program. The president of this organization recently came to town from New York or Los Angeles, I can't verify which. In fact, I can't get enough information together for a news story on the organization. As nearly as I can determine, their "facts" are heavily loaded with ultraconservative propaganda. But they do appear to be loaded with words, not bullets. I guess we can be thankful for that.

November 21, 1963—Some of Sylvia and Peter's classmates talk of tossing homemade bombs at the President of the United States when he visits us tomorrow. The worst is that most teachers do nothing to discourage this kind of adolescent madness. Many of the Dallas educators do not care for liberal political ideas.

I have heard a couple of hate-filled anti-Catholic sermons preached from the pulpit of "the world's largest and richest church" here in the Oak Cliff section of Dallas. Well, if hate for fellow Christians is sponsored by some churches, and schools are, at best, indifferent to the democratic principle of tolerance for differing political views, what can be expected from the generation of high school young adults? . . . I will be covering the Presidential motorcade from downtown, about Lamar and Elm Streets. Then I'll try to beat the motorcade to the Trade Mart where Kennedy will speak. I'm worried. More than a little.

Had I just added the cool, clear water of political reality to the pre-mix of hate propaganda labeled "Hang the Traitor," I would have had the most probable destiny of John F. Kennedy reconstituted. The political reality at that time was the schism in the Texas Democratic party which made it *necessary* for the President to come to Texas and parade through the streets of Dallas, the most dangerous place in the world for him to be at that particular time.

I still had not learned my lessons on how to predict the news when, a few days later, Dallas Police Chief Jess Curry announced at a press conference the exact time that Lee Harvey Oswald would be transferred from the city to the county jail in order to accommodate the radio and television news networks. My wife, Ruth, was reading her hunches the way I should have been.

November 23, 1963—Ruth seems to be getting a bit hysterical, which isn't at all like her. When I got home tonight, she was in quite a state because Captain Curry had announced on a televised press conference the time of Oswald's transfer to the county jail. "Someone will kill him," she said. Having attended the conference, I assured her that the announcement was undoubtedly a "decoy." Captain Curry has always shown the press the greatest consideration. However, he has also shown himself a good police officer. It is his sworn duty to protect his prisoners. I assured her that Lee Oswald would be safely in a maximum security cell at the county jail quite early tomorrow morning, long before the announced time of his transfer. Any other action on the part of Chief Curry would be madness.

November 24, 1963—I'm tired. Tired of madness. Tired of stupidity. Bone-tired from month-long days and seconds of sleep. Tired of trying to fathom this community in which I have lived for almost two years.

The press from all over the world has crowded into our little press room in city hall. Reporters rush in to telephone their stories in seven different languages. One consolation—I am no longer alone in trying to fathom why things happen in Dallas that are too "far out" to have happened anywhere, really.

Like the Big Story today. I was so certain that Oswald would be transferred in secret at an early hour to the county jail that I checked in there first thing. I learned to my horror that he had not been transferred and that he *would* be escorted out of city hall with full radio, television, and newspaper coverage, as announced! I learned, in fact, that the police and sheriff's offices were so worried that he would be shot that they had alerted Parkland Hospital to stand by and had ordered an ambulance! But they didn't switch the time for the transfer!!

I could not escape the thought that official Dallas was arranging an old time western vigilante execution for Lee Harvey Oswald. And then I saw it! I saw the angry young man who I'd felt compassion for the night before walking between two homicide detectives I knew. I saw Jack Ruby, the boisterous police buff who had bought me a cup of coffee in the pressroom the night before, walk *in front* of one of the detectives, right up to Lee Oswald, with a gun in his right hand, and shoot the young man in cold blood. One of the detectives guarding Oswald did not even try to unbutton his coat! The other, who had his coat unbuttoned, did not even reach for his gun. They *must* have seen Ruby coming. The television director did (he cued a cameraman to a closeup shot of Ruby advancing with a gun in his hand). So did the newspaper photographers. So did I, for that matter . . .

The events of that great American tragedy finally simmered down from chaos to merely a hectic pace. I got a little more sleep and a little more perspective on the current of that historical episode. I began to sense how present events were warping future events. The change of venue hearing for Jack Ruby was coming up and it seemed that his trial would most certainly be moved from the bizarre atmosphere of Dallas. A change of venue can always be obtained on the slightest legal provocation. The "logical" prediction would be for the removal of the trial from Dallas; nearly everyone thought it a foregone conclusion, including Ruby's famous lawyer, Melvin Belli. I predicted otherwise. I could sense that the Ruby trial was no longer legal business, but show business.

January 22, 1964—The big thing in Dallas now is the upcoming trial of Jack Ruby. Already it is beginning to take on the shape of the Biggest Show on Earth. Judge Joe Brown has hired a press agent . . . Jack Ruby is writing his memoirs (Ruby has retained a ghost writer to turn out little articles for the press . . .).

A great actor, Melvin Belli, will star in this extravaganza! Mr. Belli is in for a surprise. In a telephone interview with me the other day he indicated great confidence in Judge Brown's good judicial sense and was sure the trial would be transferred out of Dallas. Little does he know Dallas! What? Move it to Fort Worth? Houston? San Antonio? El Paso? Dallas would sooner be bombed out of existence! Mr. Belli has much to learn about Dallas. His lesson, I'm afraid, will be painful. Already he is becoming the villain of the piece. And he said something in the interview which I feel was quite prophetic—"If the trial is held in Dallas, you couldn't get any kind of jury except the kind that would say, 'Sure, we'll give him a fair trial, then hang him!' "

I didn't tell Mr. Belli that that was exactly what Dallas planned to do. This will get Dallas off the hook, they figure. Hang Ruby and presto, no more need to feel guilty!

But Jack Ruby will not hang. As the court of Judge Brown fails to realize, it is trying a man for murder in its efforts to acquit Dallas of its guilt, and in its own childish way it will commit enough reversible errors that the appellate court will have to set him free. He will then, in all probability, get shot before he reaches the sidewalks of Austin, Texas. There are those who have vowed to "get Ruby" if he should go free. Any phone calls to the local police authorities to this effect will be ignored. So be it.

I was more oracle than I realized at that time. Jack Ruby, of course, did not die where my "hunch" told me he would die. My hunch told me Jack Ruby would also be assassinated. I assumed this would take place after his appeal to the appellate court in Austin, Texas. He actually died of a pulmonary embolism on January 3, 1967 in Parkland Hospital in Dallas, Texas, where he was a cancer patient. But I was reading a future news story several years away. From that distance details are not that easy to read. But details can always be sketched in at the last minute. Your hunches will tell you how to be in the right place at the right time, and what the drift of the story is likely to be. Much can be put down on paper ahead of time, and that contributes greatly to the speed with which you are able to report a fast-breaking news story.

I usually have a story or two written and in my pocket when I arrive on the scene. Most of the time they furnish ninety percent of the written material I need for my first reports. In many instances, there are only two or three ways a news story can "turn out" anyway.

Take the Jack Ruby trial. There were only three possible verdicts the jury could return. While the jury was deliberating, I had plenty of time to write three good stories on the outcome of the trial. When the verdict was read one of those stories stood up without so much as a change in a comma. As a result my news service had the story and had it out to their affiliated stations around the world a good fifteen minutes before any other news service was able to break the story.

All I did was add the water of my hunches to the premix supplied by history.

Waiting for Godot

In his existentialist play, *Waiting For Godot,* Samuel Beckett had his characters waiting all through the performance for an entity who never showed. There were many ways and many times Godot was supposed to come, but he never made it in any way, at any time. One left the theater doubting that this Godot character ever existed in the first place.

There are many interpretations of the meaning of this delightful little play. The broadcast newsperson cannot help but interpret it as very good symbolic representation of the situation faced by the outside reporter cooling his heels in the pressroom, on the sidewalk, cruising in the mobile news unit, or any of the hundred other places we also serve who only sit and wait.

Developing the news story on the outside beat often leaves one with the feeling that no news stories ever existed on that beat in the first place. But they do and there is a technique for getting them to come your way. These techniques involve *preparation* and *organization.*

Homework—It Pays To Be a Renaissance Man

Preparation means you have done your homework. There is no substitute for doing homework. This involves reading the daily newspapers in your community to stay on top of everything that happens on a daily basis. Some newspapers are better than others, of course, but all generally have larger news gathering staffs and facilities than do individual broadcasting stations. Homework also includes weekly reading, from cover to cover, of one of the weekly news magazines devoted to national and international news. Read everything. Especially those things you think you are not interested in, or wouldn't read if you were just a plain civilian reading for information and entertainment. Read the sports news and the science news and the book reviews—everything. Be especially alert for people in the news who may suddenly show up in your community. Find out how they pronounce their names. If you read everything in a good daily newspaper every day and everything in a good weekly news magazine every week, you won't miss much.

Keep in mind that the earth has shrunk to the size of a village and we all belong to the same tribe now. Little is "foreign" or remote from your community. It is usually local news and it will relate to your job whether you are the do-it-all reporter-newscaster on Uncle Ezra's ten watter in Peoria or the city council special reporter on WBIG's 50,000 watter in Chicago.

To round out your homework, when you are not reading the news, ask questions of all the public officials you can find. Get to know them, their backgrounds, their opinions and biases, and whether they prefer coffee, tea, or milk, and if coffee how do they take it? Cream and sugar? Or black? Keep in mind that public officials, especially elected officials, are servants of the public—and the public is you and the people who depend upon you for the news. You really cannot get too nosey about these folks.

While you are taking in and storing away all the information you can get, don't overlook your friends and neighbors. You do not get nosey about their personal lives, of course, that is none of your business. But what they think, the opinions they hold about public officials and issues, is your business. Listen especially to opinions and ideas that differ from your own. This is the old Indian trick of one ear to the ground—it will tip you off in advance about who is sneaking up on city hall and how long before the issues break into pictures, sound, and print.

Finally, preparation means having your equipment, portable audio and video recorders, ready to roll on a few seconds notice. Fresh batteries and fresh cassettes should always be within reach. Be as unobtrusive as possible with your equipment, but be ready to snap on your eyes and/or your ears quickly. If you work with an engineer, or cameraperson, or other helper, be sure this person has everything you think you may need handy and wound up, ready to roll.

How To Get Organized—This Week

Organization means knowing where you are going to be and what you are going to do next, and next after that. It means keeping to a regular schedule as much as possible and getting back on schedule as rapidly as possible when you are thrown off. Give yourself as many coffee breaks as you like, but take them with someone who knows something you don't know and use the break to find out about it.

In any community there are a minimum of four beats that need to be organized and covered: the county court house, city or town hall, the police beat, and the organized neighborhood groups.

You may be the only outside reporter covering them all or you may be one of many outside reporters covering just a portion of one. It doesn't really matter as far as being organized is concerned. You must cover all the bases on a regular schedule. Never assume that nothing is happening across the hall. Go over there and see, or telephone over there, at least. "Waiting for Godot" can get deadly dull but that goes with the territory. The very day you figure you will skip *that* office today because nothing has happened there for the last sixteen days, is the very day the Great Pumpkin will appear in that office. Like the old-fashioned cop on the beat you stay on your feet and try every door, even if the ol' neighborhood hasn't had anything but drunks in the doorway for the last ten years.

You will find that the more often and the more regularly you come around to find out what's going on, the more you will flatter the officials you are keeping track of. They can't help but get the idea they must be important people to be visited by or called by a newsperson so often. You will make some friends among the court clerks, the mayor's secretary, the community center director. They will become your allies in keeping the public informed. And if something big appears about to break you will be the first to know. I hate to sound like Pollyanna, but it's true: perseverence pays off for the outside reporter.

We are all, at all times, waiting for Godot to come in the guise of that sudden disaster—the tornado, the flood, the explosion, the sniper in the tower, the bomber at the airport. It's a long wait, and it would be wonderful if, as in the play, this brand of Godot should never come, but sooner or later, this brand always does come to each and every community. You will find organizations in your community all set with disaster plans—the Red Cross, the Civil Defense, Civil Air Patrol people, and hospital emergency room staff. Get together with these organizations before any disaster ever happens. On a calm and sunny day find out exactly what their plans are. Try your own hand at figuring out the next disaster to hit your community. Let your intuition speak to you in hunches, especially if you have lived in the community a while. You'll be surprised what your mind has picked up on a subliminal level. Put your regular senses to work, also. Is it about time for that hundred-year flood next spring? Is your city loaded with chemical plants manufacturing poisons by the tank car load? Is your small town on the main line of a railroad with a rusty switch just waiting for a tank car of chlorine to stumble over? How's your airport rated by the pilots who regularly fly in and out? Is it one where they cross themselves before each and every landing?

We said in a previous chapter that no news story breaks out of the blue. Your community's next disaster will have its booby trap primed and set *somewhere*. Make your plans for how you are going to cover it early on.

I have evolved one simple master plan for covering disasters large and small. I discovered this marvelous master plan one day when I was trapped in a hospital emergency room by a hurricane. After a brief period of fretting because I couldn't get out into the wild winds and witness the destruction first hand, I suddenly found all the news flowing in to me through the big double doors of the ambulance entrance—the dead and the injured, the actual eyewitnesses from all parts of the coast. Luckily, my communications held up (the hospital had done some good planning) and for many hours I was the only reporter with contact to my newsroom. I learned a lot from that experience. I learned not to go fighting my way to the scene of a disaster, any disaster, even a four-alarm fire. After all, the *scene* of a disaster is just that and nobody there ever seems to know what happened anyway. Stories are always conflicting and mostly exaggerated. At the hospital emergency room the scope of a disaster can be assessed very quickly. This is where the people who were most affected by the disaster will arrive. Some, of course are in no condition to be interviewed. But I find that many are. And it is the people and what the disaster has done to their lives that make the stories.

When President Kennedy was killed in Dallas, the drama was played in the emergency room of Parkland Hospital. All the principals were there. All the news came walking and rushing through the big double doors. If one could only be in one place, this was the place.

In another situation I got an excellent report on a big fire that did millions of dollars in damage but injured no one except one fireman who had cut his finger. By being at the hospital emergency room I got the only really coherent story of the fire from him while he was getting his finger stitched up. Reporters who went to the fire had a hard time finding anyone who wasn't too busy to talk to!

My simple master plan for covering any disaster is to go to the emergency room of the nearest hospital, usually a city or county general, and let the news all come to me. And somehow, the visual imagery of that grimy, disheveled fireman sitting on a table in the emergency room and getting his finger stitched by a doctor while telling the story of the fire had more dramatic impact than all your color footage of billowing smoke and flickering flames. If you have ENG equipment, you are able to get the best coverage because you can tape people reacting to the disaster.

It works for me—this way of waiting for Godot.

6

The Green Eyeshade

In direct contrast to outside reporting, working inside the broadcast newsroom is not a matter of waiting for anybody or anything. It all presses in on you. The incessant teletype machines never let up. The telephone, the red "hot line," is always ringing or blinking if its bell has been silenced—the latest feed from the network is coming up—someone just has to see you to hand you their latest press release in person—tape has to be dubbed and carted, radio or TV it makes little difference. In the television newsroom deadlines are usually spaced farther apart than in the radio newsroom, but there is a lot more material to be processed in between times—the rat cage spins no more slowly! But whatever name the newsperson in charge inside the spinning cage is called, the job to be done is editing. So, inherit the green eyeshade.

The editor is the one who decides what stories to broadcast and in what sequence. Someone has to make these decisions for every five-minute radio newscast and every fifteen- or thirty-minute or one-hour TV newscast. How does one assess news values? Why is one story "more important" than another story? What story does one lead off with when the "on air" light goes on? The answers to all those questions have highly subjective answers that deal with an elusive thing called "editorial judgment."

The development of editorial judgment comes with experience and familiarity with one's medium. It also has to do with the kind of journalism one believes in. In broadcast journalism one makes those editorial judgments with one green-glinting eye on the numbers game in which one's station is always embroiled.

Every Day is Judgment Day

What can I tell you about how to make editorial judgments? Perhaps it will be most helpful to share with you the experience I had which taught me the most about exercising editorial judgment in the structuring of news broadcasts. I was actually called "Senior Editor" on this job, and I had the responsibility for structuring 32 fifteen-minute radio newscasts that were broadcast one right after the other from 1:00 p.m. to 9:00 p.m. on WNUS, Chicago, the nation's first all-news radio station. There were three of us senior editors working eight-hour shifts.

We each had three other on-air newscasters. Every newscaster did one fifteen-minute newscast per hour during the eight-hour shift. There were no features, no "magazine pieces," no interview programs, no religious programs on Sunday morning—just one fifteen-minute newscast after another, twenty-four hours a day, seven days a week. There were three commercial breaks in each newscast and one commercial break between each newscast—a maximum of eighteen commercial breaks per hour. We did this for three years. I figure I compiled more than 28,000 fifteen-minute newscasts, delivering about one-fourth of them, or some 7,000 myself, on the air. Our consumption of hard news was copious.

To feed this monster we had almost every service of almost every wire service in existence. The news came in on fourteen teletype machines, including one city wire that covered nothing but Chicago metropolitan news. Several state wires gave us regional news from Illinois, Indiana, Wisconsin, and Michigan—the four-state area we served—plus we had sports wire and weather wire. The rest were the usual national and international wires that serve all newspapers and radio and television stations. On each shift there was one outside reporter and one rewrite person. Our production engineer would take the feeds from the international audio services cart and cue them ready to go on the air. The engineer also taped telephone conversations with the news-makers tracked down by our newscasters between broadcasts. When a newsperson was not on the air, he was on the telephone. Each newsperson had the option of airing his own "exclusives" on his own newscast before it was used as a routine item in subsequent newscasts.

We got some good ones. The evening New York City blacked out, shortly after dusk, one of my crew tracked down Governor Nelson Rockefeller aboard his private plane just dropping down into Kennedy Airport and talked with the Governor on the phone as his plane was landing. Another got through to the radar operator at Tinker Air Force Base in Oklahoma City the night hundreds of unidentified flying objects "invaded" Texas, Oklahoma, and New Mexico, and got a reading on the fantastic altitude, speed, and maneuvering ability of the objects before the Air Force brass got wind of his report and cut it off. We had exciting times. And we did, I think, push the radio medium to its limits for nearly instantaneous, continuous news reporting from the streets of Chicago to the streets of Moscow.

One day I made a startling discovery. This editorial judgment we were talking about—and which we senior editors always agonized over—could all be resolved on the basis of redundancy! One could even program a computer to make one's editorial judgments and structure one's newscasts! It was one of those things that once thought of seems perfectly obvious. Boiled down to one of "Mike's Laws" it reads like this: *The greater the redundancy the bigger the story and the higher it ranks in the structure of the newscasts.*

The night of the New York City-East Coast blackout, I and most of my afternoon crew stayed over to help the night crew cover the story. At one point during the evening, when I made the rounds of the teletype machines, every single machine was typing out a story related to the blackout, including the sports wire, the Chicago local wire, and the weather wire. I flipped my monitor through the six telephone "hot lines," which were in simultaneous use by our news people and reporters, and all were having conversations related to the black out! No doubt about what the lead story would be on the next upcoming newscast. In fact, for several hours all the news in all the newscasts were blackout stories. After that experience I became far less subjective about my editorial judgments.

One does not, of course, normally have the opportunity to observe directly the redundancy that occurs in a newsroom equipped as was WNUS in its heyday. But one can still play the game with only one teletype machine and one telephone line. The trick is to imagine how widely reported a story is at the time one is putting together a newscast. Is it the kind of story likely to be picked up in Chicago and New York? London and Mozambique? Is it a meaningful story for people in Peoria and New Delhi? Or is it a story only of interest to the east side of Indianapolis, Indiana?

Pick the story most likely to be reported most widely at the time your newscast is to be aired and scale down to the weather from there. Instant editorial judgment!

This, of course, is one of those rules made to be broken, but it does serve well when in doubt. It gives one a feeling of confidence when under the green eyeshade that there is a useful frame of reference from which to structure an interesting newscast on radio or television.

One may well want to go with that Indianapolis story as the lead for any number of very good reasons. I often lead a newscast with the weather story when I feel maybe my audience would like to be assured that their weekend picnic will be blessed by sunshine, before they get their spirits dampened by the latest scandal breaking in Washington, even if it is being reported in Tokyo at the time. But even then I find, if I analyze the rest of my newscast, I have pretty much gone from the most redundant to the least redundant stories.

Making use of the wire service editors' consensus judgment, or imagined consensus judgment, serves well for making quick rat-cage editorial judgments during the day-to-day whirl of news editing. What about stories that are important, but no one realizes just *how* important? Are there such stories? How do discrimination and judgment enter into covering such stories?

There are many stories that are important because of their potential for future impact on your audience. Such a story surfaced in 1974 in an issue of *Science,* a weekly journal respected and read by most professional scientists. In that issue there appeared an open letter from a group of prominent molecular biologists *asking their colleagues to defer certain experiments and to perform others with extreme caution!*

As far as I know, this event was unprecedented in human history. Certainly, such a thing had never happened before in the history of science. Yet, it was hardly a media event. In spite of the fact that *Science* is read cover to cover every week by reporters for all major news media (as part of their homework), it was sparsely reported as a "moratorium" (which it was not) on some rather esoteric genetic technology. But the event, the letter in *Science,* set off a chain reaction in the public sector. Senator Edward M. Kennedy read it and convened his subcommittee on health for public hearings. The regents at the University of Michigan read it and halted construction on a laboratory designed to conduct such research. Thirty other members of Congress read it and immediately ordered their Technology Assessment Board to review the research. Skirmishes broke out between community activists and scientists in New Haven, Bloomington, and San Diego. Hearings were held by the New York attorney general's office. The National Institutes of Health and the Environmental Protection Agency were galvanized into action to try to regulate the research. Reverberations bounced from Pennsylvania Avenue to Downing Street to the Kremlin. The governments of Great Britain and the Soviet Union pounced on their scientists who were engaged in this area of microbiology research which uses sleight of hand with DNA to teach old bugs new tricks.

Why was this story so important that it deserved every bit as much coverage as the moon landing or the Watergate scandal? Because here was a group of scientists who had discovered a new technology that could cure us or kill us and it scared the pants off them. It's future impact on every man, woman, and child in your audience made it such a story.

But those of us of the press, and especially those of us in broadcast news tend to ignore such stories until the Andromeda strain escapes from the laboratory and the self-destruct sequence has been initiated. Only then do we think we have a story. But by then even a computer wearing the green eyeshade knows what your lead story is going to be.

What we need to do is to exercise our judgment on each and every event we witness or hear about. We must ask ourselves, "What is the potential impact of this event on the members of our news audience?" Then we discriminate between those events of little impact and those of greater impact—from that judgment and from that discrimination. Then comes the selections of stories to be reported and their sequencing in the newscast.

I have found that the science fiction writer's trick of extrapolation can often help me spot an important story about which no consensus exists or can be imagined. By extrapolating from the known facts to what might some day be, I often come to some sensible editorial judgment on the value of an event. Applied to that little burglary at the Watergate hotel after the White House connection was made, my extrapolation on that event kept it at the top of my newscasts at a time when most other broadcasters were ignoring the stories because they thought it was just Democratic political propaganda.

The structuring of the television newscast is often thought to be more difficult because of the consideration given to the availability of visual material in the making of editorial judgments. This idea can be a real live cookie-monster that, if allowed, can eat up one's editorial judgment. Of course, every effort should be made to get the best possible visual coverage on a news story that is to be aired. But it should not become an overriding obsession blinding one to the value or "weight" of a news story. After all, the news is the news is the news. Visuals in a television newscast and audio "actualities" in a radio newscast should be inserted only to the extent that they contribute to the clarity of the news being reported. Radio broadcasters, too, tend to get carried away if they have a good audio actuality on a story. The tendency is to use *that* story even though it would rank very low in their editorial judgment without the actuality. This is probably the entertainment specter come back to haunt us once again! Banish the banshee! A second-rate news story is never as interesting as a first-rate news story no matter how dressed up with pretty picture or sound. The way to go is to polish your broadcast style so that you can *tell* the news with impact and authority.

"Mister, Can You Spare A Handout?

There is another pit of deepest, darkest despair you will wish to avoid while wearing the green eyeshade. That is the pit that lurks behind the public relations facade, dug for you by those legions of individuals who would manage your news for you. Theirs is the art of the reverse panhandle. They would make beggars of us all.

Public relations people are employed in the task of trying to get their "advertising" into the body of your newscast, and on the front pages of your newspapers. They stage events and write handouts and other pablum to feed the voracious appetites of all news consuming organizations. They make a tremendous winnowing job for journalists. There are kernels in their fruits that you cannot afford to ignore, but there is also much chaff that must be carried away on the wind.

All things that come to you in the mail, or directly to the station by special messenger, or which you get handed at a news conference should be scrutinized carefully to determine what the individual or organization that wants your attention is really up to. Often what they are up to is just the opposite of what is being brought to your attention. Not that they will always lie to you. It's sometimes just a matter of emphasis. A company exploiting natural resources will always have a good "ecology program" going. The program may amount to no more than planting a hill of beans but they will focus your attention on this hill of beans so you don't notice that they are raping the garden. So if you are invited out to a bean-planting ceremony, be sure to peek behind the newly placed bean pole to see what happened to last year's crop and what is being planned for future bean crops.

Most of the handouts you get handed will be image-building gimmicks of one kind or another. Since we see our job as one of giving the public a picture of reality on which to base decisions about the running of our democracy, we must find ways to inquire into the disparity between the image being built in the mind of the public and the image that would result should the facts be known. This disparity, when exposed, forms the well-known credibility gap, so infamous in national and international politics.

At no time did this credibility gap become more obvious than with the rise and fall of the Nixon presidential administration. All the handouts said that this was a "law and order" administration. The attorney general, John Mitchell, was often referred to in the press as "Mr. Law and Order." But when the facts became known, when we had looked behind all the bean poles, we found that laws were being broken left and right. Most of the top members of this administration wound up in jail or on probation and even the president had to be pardoned for his part in the law-breaking.

The problem was that in 1972, when this administration was asking the American people to let it govern, the public had a false picture of reality presented to it by us journalists. We let the Nixon campaigners manage our news for us. We took their handouts and other pablum and fed it right on to the people without asking, "What are they *really* up to?" All but two of us failed to get the real news behind the PR facade.

From the Bay of Pigs to the retreat to San Clemente, right on through the Vietnam war, the civil rights marches, and the Student-Young People's uprisings of the sixties, we had our news nicely managed for us. A thorough study of the history of the news during the John F. Kennedy, Lyndon B. Johnson, and Richard M. Nixon administrations should be made by all of us who would avoid the pitfalls and pratfalls of reporting by handout.

Reporting at the grass roots level is no safer from the pit-traps of the PR crowd. Everything your local police officer's association hands you is not necessarily so. I have seen a local police chief go to jail for the very drug store burglary he was investigating. Handouts from the "do-good" groups should be checked out with the facts every time. The rule is universal.

Take the handout, look it over carefully for clues, toss it in the wastebasket, and then go after the story if you feel there is one worth broadcasting. This rule applies to everyone.

I believe the good reporter will not even broadcast the handout made by God on Mount Sinai without first checking for the fire in the bush.

Part III

Objectivity, delivery, and eccentricity—
not exactly the three musketeers,
but still a trio to respect.

7

Cutting Across the Bias

Fast and accurate reporting without resorting to fabrication is not possible unless one is thoroughly familiar with that mental prankster that tricks us all at times—bias.

We all have our "slants," our prejudices about any news event we happen to be reporting or writing about. This bias can stand awkwardly in the way of our hunches, too, vectoring them off in the wrong direction.

It is not possible to be "unbiased." It is possible to recognize and compensate for that bias and thus, report in an unbiased manner, or nearly so. The bias may then become an element of style, contributing to the interest of our reports but not damaging their integrity.

The detection of our own bias is not easy. We may think we know how our cloth is slanted, but unless we have actually worked a bit at self-analysis, we seldom do. As a matter of fact, our actual biases are often the opposite of what we feel we believe them to be. The key word is *believe*. Our true biases spring from our true beliefs. And our *true* beliefs are often buried under layers of rationale.

Take the situation in the medical profession in the western world, for instance. Ask almost any medical doctor if he is biased in favor of death and disease; that is, ask him if he truly believes in sickness or does he truly believe in health. Unless he is a man of unusual insight he will swear that of course he believes in health—*his bias,* he will say, is most assuredly toward life, otherwise why would he work such long hours sacrificing family life and almost all else, except money, to try to keep folks from death and cure their disease?

But on analysis we learn that each medical student is issued his own cadaver. He learns his primary lessons from the dead. And when he is finally admitted to the amphitheater of the living to peer inside the human body, it is the part of the body that is diseased that he observes being surgically removed or repaired. He is carefully taught the dogma of germ theory and he certainly believes in the reality of the bacterium and the virus. He graduates to a hospital and must reside there among the constantly ailing and dying. What he truly believes in, then, his bias, is toward death and disease. Otherwise, he could not be a successful doctor.

On the other hand, the ancient Chinese doctor who took payment from his patient only so long as the patient was well was forced by his society to have a bias that favored health. If his patient got sick, he was a bad doctor and not worthy of economic support!

It is not only the modern-day western physician who has a bias that runs counter to his rationale about his bias. We see the same situation displayed by the career military people who are biased for war, not peace. And the lawyer who is biased toward lawlessness because this is what he *truly* believes in.

Now to bring the medicine home and get ready to swallow the bitter pill. What do we broadcast journalists truly believe? Can we see in ourselves a generalized bias as we have seen in others? Does "Mike's Law" of opposites apply to himself? I'm afraid it does.

Having read this far, you must have detected my general bias *against* that which is new, or news, in the dictionary sense of ". . . never existing before, appearing . . . for the first time." My very first sentence was, "Human beings have an amazingly limited repertoire of things to be experienced!" And I believe this to be a general bias of most journalists. There is little difference between the journalist and the historian and both, I think, truly believe in the dogma of "nothing new under the sun," and "history repeats itself." And perhaps even in that ultimate nemesis to the professional journalist, "No news is good news!"

Having divined my general bias against news, I will not defend it. It is a detrimental belief. Just as I believe that a healer of human ills should be a true believer in human health, and that a military person must believe in the reality of peace on earth, just as a lawyer should believe in lawfulness, a journalist should believe that everything is new and exciting and has never happened before. He should be like a little child to whom all things are new. I am certain that if we all became as little children we would indeed enter into the journalistic heaven.

But that would be a whole new ball game. I am not at all qualified or knowledgeable about childlike journalism, though I do think it would be far more constructive for our society than what we have now.

No. I'm stuck, for better or for worse, in the old journalistic ball game. But at least I know what my general bias is and I know that it is likely to trick me into a dull, resigned "here we go again" style of reporting.

The Watergate scandal is a case in point. The reality of President Nixon's criminal activities to obstruct justice became undeniably evident, but the general journalistic bias toward nothing *really* new ever happening took charge and most of us said, "Ha! History repeats itself!" We began to usurp the historian's territory and look back into previous presidential administrations for evidence of criminal activities in our White House. The same bias inspired many editorials about the need for future checks on the administrative branch of our government. Why? Because we believed, deep down, that history was simply repeating itself and would repeat itself again. That bias tended to obscure the truly new aspects of the Watergate scandal—that we, here, in the United States of America, were for the first time in our history actually living under a totalitarian form of government. This is what the childlike view—the unbiased picture—was showing us. I shall never forget the comment of one of our Senators who said, "The hardest thing to take about the whole mess is the fact that my children were right all along!" And I am haunted by the comment made by my own child, Sylvia, which I recorded in my journal in November, 1963, at a time when none of us dreamed that Mr. Nixon had any kind of political future ahead of him, "If Richard Nixon had been elected president . . . we'd all be in jail . . . the whole country would be overrun with these Ku Kluxers like Dallas is . . ."

If I were a holy man, writing in the Book of Prophecy, I would write in very large letters, "Pay attention to what your children tell you, for only they are wise in the ways of the world!" And only they are free from the generalized journalistic bias that no new thing can happen under the sun.

In addition to the general bias, we have our special case biases that will tend to slant each and every specific news story we report.

These are harder to detect and minimize. But it can be done, and it needs to be done, as frequently and as ruthlessly as possible.

A quick reading on one's bias can be had by applying Mike's Law of Opposites—ask yourself, "What is the belief that is diametrically opposed to what I think I believe?" This may give you a clue.

I have found that the most effective method for uncovering my own biases is to look at those things I believe to be realities and question whether or not they are in fact realities, or whether they might be ideas *about* reality instead. I often accuse other people of not being "realistic." What I am saying is that they do not agree with my ideas about reality. Once I have separated my ideas about reality from others' ideas about reality I have a list of my own biases. I have come to believe that we all create our own personal reality out of the fabric of our ideas about reality.

If this is true, one cannot eliminate one's biases when reporting the news or engaging in any other human activity. But being aware of what the biases are will enable one to use them as elements of style in reporting rather than as explanatory elements likely to turn one's news report into a propaganda piece.

Never cut your news stories on the bias, then. The best and most accurate reporting is done by cutting the news story across the bias at as near to a 90° angle as you can get.

8

On the Air

Broadcast style is what enables us to sit and watch Harry Reasoner tell us about the news face to face without even being aware of the fact that no other visual material is being inserted to "illustrate" the news. Broadcast style is what keeps us glued to the radio when Paul Harvey does his fifteen-minute newscast without a single actuality or other voice intrusion. In fact, it is the lack of broadcast style that makes us yearn for and lean on such crutches in the first place. But there is no substitute for broadcast style.

As near as we can tie it down, broadcast style involves a manner or mode of expression in language; a way of putting thoughts into words. It involves distinction, excellence, originality, and character in broadcast expression.

How do we get it? How do we improve upon it? How can we develop such style that listeners and viewers will sit enthralled with only our own presence on camera, or behind the microphone, and curse the break for commercials because it takes us away from them?

Or, less ambitiously, but perhaps more answerable, how can we say what we have to say and get people to watch and listen?

As applied to the news, broadcast style appears to have its genesis in one's ability to speak with authority—not to be an authority but to speak with authority. Walter Cronkite was not an authority on space travel, but when he reported on the Apollo missions he spoke with a great deal of authority. The distinction, excellence, and originality of his reporting quite obviously stemmed from a great interest in what he was doing. He had a vast store of general knowledge about the subject. He had experience, having previously reported the Mercury and Gemini missions, and he had done his homework. His manner or mode of expression reflected his fascination with the subject, and gave him his character—his style.

One cannot speak with authority without understanding what one is speaking about. This is the bottom line of broadcast style. When one reads a news story from teleprompter or wire copy one must understand exactly what the copy says. This understanding comes from one's general store of knowledge about the subject matter of the copy. It comes from previous experience of reporting on that or similar stories. It comes from having done one's homework.

The most that I can tell you about broadcast style is to become a generalist, one who knows a little bit about a lot of things rather than a specialist who only knows a lot about a little bit. This will enable you to understand most anything you read and thereby give your rendition a ring of authority.

It is particularly important to keep up with currently developing news stories and learn their background. This will keep you in command as you report subsequent developments.

It is also necessary to develop an interest in your subject matter. A newsperson or reporter should have an interest in everything. If this interest can grow into a fascination for the subject matter, so much the better.

Act Like a Journalist!

One cannot pretend or "put on" this interest and fascination. This never works. Your audience will sense this every time. This is not to say you cannot apply *acting* techniques to your work in order to achieve an authoritative delivery. Acting is not pretending. Acting is understanding and living a part. An actor must have a deep understanding of his lines, of the copy he reads, in order to read interpretively, which means with the aura of authority.

One late spring day, I was listening to tapes and going over the usual pile of resumes from students just graduated from the University of Texas School of Journalism. I was looking for a likely candidate for our intern program when I heard a tape I couldn't believe. This young woman's voice spoke about the news with authority. She sounded as if she had had a great deal of experience, and yet her resumé listed no jobs in broadcast news, although she had had considerable experience as a cook and bartender-cocktail waitress while working her way through school. Her only broadcast experience was the little she got in connection with her broadcast journalism courses at the university.

When she came in for her interview I told her quite frankly that I had never heard one so inexperienced sound so much like an experienced news broadcaster. I told her I found it hard to believe. She then "confessed" that she considered herself to be an actress and had had a great deal of training and experience in theater. What she did, she said, was to play the role of a broadcast journalist. She applied her acting techniques and talents to the role and played it convincingly.

I hired her and encouraged her to continue to play the role of broadcast journalist and to develop her style with her acting techniques. In playing the role of a broadcast journalist she became a broadcast journalist of exceptional ability—she had become "type cast."

I had not realized, until reflection upon this experience, the part acting had played in my own career as a broadcast journalist. The small college I attended as an undergraduate had no broadcast or journalism department but it did have a good department of speech and drama. I worked as a staff announcer at the local radio station while focusing on drama in my academic work. I made no conscious effort to apply what I learned in acting and theater work to my daily radio work or to the fifteen-minute newscasts I would "rip and read" from the news wire. But only one year out of college and with just three years of local station experience I managed to pass the CBS network audition and get a job with a basic CBS station. The producer who supervised my audition told me I got the job in spite of my youth because of the authoritative way I had read the news portion of the audition.

In retrospect I am sure it was application of acting techniques and my courses in interpretive reading that turned the trick. I was not, certainly, at that time a journalist. It was only after I was assigned to the job of reading a nightly newscast on the southeastern leg of the CBS network that I went down to the local university and enrolled in some courses in journalism. Even this act was a follow-through effort to "learn the part"—to learn what a journalist was and does so I could be more effective in my nightly role as newscaster when that "on the air" light signaled that the curtain had been raised on my role as broadcast journalist. At that time, 1945, there was no requirement that a radio newscaster know anything about journalism.

If broadcast style has its genesis in one's ability to speak with authority, its final revelation comes from one's understanding of the meaning of the news and the effect the news has on the individual who first hears about it from you. After all, that individual is probably more interested in himself/herself than in anything else, so you can get a lot more attention by addressing your viewer/listener personally. Many of the best broadcast journalists make this thesis an important element of their style.

"Your weather is going to be nice tomorrow . . ."

"Your utility bill is going up another notch next month, thanks to . . ."

"Your President is haranguing Congress for a tax break . . ."

"Some of your scientists are apparently frightened out of their wits that our new technology for stacking your deck of DNA cards will blow the intricate genetic balance that keeps all your chips in the game . . ."

This is what I call "the news belongs to everyone syndrome" and it is a very effective broadcast style.

Another effective style is the good news/bad news sandwich. The late radio news commentator Gabriel Heater made this style famous with his lead-in, "There's good news tonight . . ." He often gave us a lot of bad news, too, especially in the early days of World War II, but there was always some good news to balance the bad. I am sure that most people will watch and listen more attentively to the bad news we often have to report if we look around for some good news to give them at the same time. In fact, when the news is bad we tend to concentrate on that and overlook the good things happening along with it. This puts the bad news out of perspective and destroys the contrast so essential to that picture of reality our audience must have if they are to make their self-governing decisions intelligently. A broadcast style built around the good news/bad news sandwich not only makes for popularity, it performs a very real service to our profession.

Humor is an important element of broadcast style that also serves to keep human events in perspective. Harry Reasoner builds his very effective style around a droll humor and a twinkling of the eye. The probing and needling styles of Barbara Walters and Mike Wallace are important elements in their abilities to capture and hold an audience for the news.

All of these styles and their elements have a common denominator. News listeners like these styles because they come to feel that the broadcast journalist not only knows what is going on, but how what is going on is going to affect them as individuals. We are all unique human beings and so, perhaps, our best broadcast style will have to evolve out of this humanity.

The wisdom accumulated by the human race so far would seem to indicate that the essence of humanity is the ability to love. Eric Fromm, in *The Art of Loving*, has characterized love as consisting of four elements: care, concern, respect, and knowledge. It would seem to me that the journalist desiring to develop his broadcast style out of his heritage as a human being would have to come to really care about the news—care about the events in human experience he chooses to report. He will need to learn to feel concern for those he reports to, and respect them as individuals. And he will have to have knowledge of their cares and concerns as well as knowledge of what is happening in his community and in his world that is going to affect them.

Perhaps an effective style emerges in the personality of the broadcaster when he has learned to some degree to love and feel at one with his brothers and sisters.

Our broadcast style will always accurately reflect our raison d'être.

9

Inside Lou Grant

Edward Asner, an actor who for years played the role of Lou Grant, news director, on the Mary Tyler Moore television series, personified the grass roots journalist-turned-news director, even among news directors themselves. It wasn't unusual to often find Asner at a national gathering of news directors. In fact, I think all of us who are or have been news directors feel that someone important is missing from our gathering if "Lou Grant" doesn't show up.

Asner studied his part so well, and played it so convincingly, that he could step into an actual job as news director and do the job quite effectively. He knew more about what a news director is and does, and more about how to be one than many working news directors. Why? Because he took more time to study the job than most "real" news directors.

It does take the study techniques of the actor to define the role of news director. If we look inside Lou Grant, we can perhaps define this role more clearly as it is played out in the day-to-day operation of a broadcast news department.

Even if one doubles in the role of newscaster, reporter, producer or anchorperson, the role of news director is a separate function and should be kept that way. If you are the news director of a one-person news department, this separation has to be maintained if you are to be effective in the role of director of the news. In this case you will find that you talk to yourself a lot—that's fine. It will help to keep the role isolated, even if you are also the producer, writer, and the anchorperson.

The first thing we notice as we take a close look at Lou Grant is that the Peter Principle does not apply. In his book*, *The Peter Principle,* Dr. Laurence J. Peter states that his analysis of hundreds of cases of occupational incompetence leads him to formulate the following:

> In a hierarchy every employee tends to rise to his level of incompetence . . . My Principle is the key to an understanding of all hierarchal systems, and therefore to an understanding of the whole structure of civilization. A few eccentrics try to avoid getting involved with hierarchies, but everyone in business, industry, trade unionism, politics, government, the armed forces, religion, and education are so involved. All of them are controlled by the Peter Principle.

> Many of them, to be sure, may win a promotion or two, moving from one level of competence to a higher level of competence. But competence in that new position qualifies them for still another promotion. For each individual, for *you,* for *me,* the final promotion is from a level of competence to a level of incompetence.

The scariest thing about becoming a competent broadcast journalist is that one is likely to be promoted to news director, and this is another ball game—one in which you can get stuck if it turns out to be your level of incompetence. If it turns out that you are competent as a news director, then you face the hazard of a further promotion upward and onward in the hierarchy until you either get smart and defeat the Peter Principle by practicing Creative Incompetence, or until the system defeats you by promoting you to your real level of incompetency.

That is why a careful look at the news director's position is essential for any competent broadcast journalist who really enjoys his/her job. You will get all kinds of clues about practicing creative incompetence and thus avoiding the slings and arrows of the outrageous fortune of promotion in the hierarchy of broadcasting. We often see in Lou Grant the sad nostalgia from his earlier days as a reporter with the *Detroit Free Press,* and his joy at having been a successful TV journalist. As news director, Lou Grant was no longer able to go where the action was—or even spend much time in the newsroom itself, where the action becomes a news broadcast.

*The Peter Principle, Laurence J. Peter and Raymond Hull. Copyright 1969 by William Morrow & Company, Inc., 105 Madison Avenue, New York, New York 10016.

As news director, like Lou Grant, you will spend most of your time in an office doing paper work. This can be highly frustrating. If you are lucky enough not to have an assignments editor, you can sometimes get a piece of the action by making this a part of your job. You can figure out where the action is likely to be and make sure you have someone there to cover it. Scheduling is an important part of the news director's job.

If your own personal budgeting problems are not challenge enough, or if your spouse takes care of this, you may enjoy the game of making financial ends meet in the news department. There is never enough money available for the people and the equipment you need to hold on to your competitive position in the market, to say nothing of rising above it. If you have a good head for figures and an eye for thrift, though, you may be able to bring home high marks in economics.

Most reporters do well in the personnel management aspects of the news director's job when they get promoted. It takes a thick skin to be a reporter, and the armor serves well when firing people who are doing outstanding jobs because budgets have been cut or because the manager's wife doesn't like the impertinence of "that new news-girl"—the very impertinence that gave you the scoop on the mayor's mistress! A thick skin comes in handy, too, when hiring people, since you are usually able to offer them only about half of what you know they are worth.

Perhaps you enjoy keeping records—personnel records, inventories on teletype paper and ribbons, supplies, telephone calls, gas mileage—that kind of thing. If one has the instincts of a quartermaster, this can be appealing.

If you enjoy bathroom humor and long, nearly pointless stories about a wide variety of trivia, you may be able to tolerate the endless rounds of staff meetings in good spirits. (Just don't expect the spirits to be passed around to dull the pain.) Although if you enjoy haggling, bargaining, and tripped-out egos, you may enjoy the meatier moments of these meetings.

Handling a telephone comes naturally to any ex-newsperson-turned-news director, so you may be in your element during those long harangues from your favorite constant-replier-to-controversial-news-items as you explain for the forty-fifth time that you can give equal time to reply to an editorial but not to a news item from the Associated Press. This, of course, will be only one of the many types of telephone calls that will be switched over to your desk.

Many news directors, like Lou Grant, really dig the personal problems of their staff that they often are called on to help solve—that is great. Most have a good background in sympathetic listening from their reporting days. It is a fine and constructive part of the job and requires no previous vows of chastity or poverty. While you cannot expect to make the fifty or so bucks an hour charged by the professionals in that business, these problems are often more effectively solved by head-banging than by head-shrinking—gentle head-banging, naturally, in the Lou Grant manner.

Now that you know what goes on behind that door marked "Lou Grant, News Director," you can decide whether or not you wish to go about your job as a broadcast journalist in a good and competent manner and run the risk of being promoted to news director, or, as Hamlet said, ". . . take arms against a sea of troubles and by opposing end them . . .," which in contemporary terms means practicing creative incompetence.

In case you think that you can simply refuse the promotion to news director when it comes and continue working happily in your job of gathering, reporting, and producing, let me assure you that this is too simplistic an approach. Dr. Peter warns about this in his book. He calls it "Peter's Parry" and says that it does not pay, unless you are unmarried with no close relatives and few friends.

I found that Peter's Parry does not work even under those conditions. I am married and I do have close relatives and lots of friends. However, they are all exceptionally understanding of my eccentricities about not getting involved with hierarchies. When the news director of the radio station for which I was working from noon to six as afternoon newsperson left (to get back to news reporting in another city) I was asked to take his job. Knowing that my family and friends would understand and not bug me about the money and "opportunity" I was turning down, I told the station manager, "Thank you very much, but I like the job I have now and it gives me the freedom to write articles and stories and other foolish things." The crafty manager appeared sympathetic to my cause, and asked that I take the job as "acting" news director until he could find a replacement. I foolishly agreed. I was "acting" news director for this station for five years! At one point I was even in danger of being put in charge of news operations for the station owner's whole chain of stations! It was then that I did a quick study on the art of inventive incompetence. I finally got out of the news director's job by raising my salary to the point where the station could no longer afford me. It was an agonizing way to go.

As Dr. Peter himself admits, Peter's Parry is impracticable for most people.

What is needed if you are to avoid the dreaded promotion to administrative obscurity is to be inventive in ways of creating the impression that you have already reached your level of incompetence. These techniques of inventive incompetence will work wonders if you choose an area in which to work them that does not directly hinder you in carrying out the main duties of your present healthy, happy work of broadcast journalism. These are all tested and tried techniques worked out by me or by some of my fellow Peter Groupies or by the master, Dr. Peter, himself. You may exhibit one or more of the following symptoms of higher placement.

Nobody quite trusts a news director who shows a penchant for niggling, officious economy. So switch off lights, turn thermostats up in the summer and down in the winter to "save energy." Pick up paper clips off the floor and fish them out of wastebaskets, all the while muttering homilies on the value of thrift. (Ben Franklin offers a wealth of excellent quotes for this ploy.) Refuse to kick in to the coffee fund, and bring your own thermos coffee instead. Bring your lunch in a paper sack if others go out for lunch. Be standoffish about station social affairs—just enough to create a little bit of suspicion and distrust should your name come up as a possible news director.

The ploy that kept me from the job of administering a chain of news departments is a good one. You might find it useful in certain instances. I always parked my news car in the space reserved for the station's owner, whenever he was in town visiting. I also grew a beard when the station was programming for the country music bunch. Then, when they switched to "progressive" country and all the DJ's grew hair on their faces, I shaved mine off. You have to be sensitive to the times.

The wearing of unconventional clothes is a useful technique to send out the message that you are already working at your level of incompetence. I recommend eschewing any hint of western clothing if you work for a country music radio station, but cowboy boots and Stetson hats are good if the station is a middle-of-the-roader or easy listener. The cowboy garb is good if you are trying to avoid promotion at a metropolitan TV station.

Female newspersons trying to avoid the promotion trap might try a bit too much or too little makeup and the *occasional* wearing of inappropriate dress and hair style. Very strong perfume and bright, noisy jewelry also works well, especially around a television station.

These are just some ideas that may help you develop your own incompetence inventions. Keep in mind the importance of concealing the fact that you want to avoid being made news director. It is well to grumble a bit to your peers in the newsroom about not getting the promotion when you do succeed in being passed over for it.

In the event you are a news director and you like it that way, you can, of course, develop techniques to avoid going up that next dangerous notch by exhibiting one or more of the symptoms of final achievement. As B.M. Baruch has advised, "Always do one thing less than you think you can do." That bit of sage advice will keep you from making that final move upward onto your true plateau of incompetence.

And now, here is a final word from the sponsor of this chapter, Edward Asner. Sitting at the bar during a break at a recent gathering of radio and television news directors, he swirled the ice in his martini around and around and, looking very Lou Grantish, said, "You know, if I really was in this business I'd never be a news director. I'd move up horizontally to reporting bigger and better news stories!"

You may take that with a twist of lemon.

Part IV

Pictures, Sound and Fury.

10

What Radio Did Before the Camera Came

The broadcast medium has a split personality. While broadcast news is broadcast news is broadcast news, as Gertrude Stein might have said, it is broadcast in one of two media—one "hot" and the other "cool." Television, the cool one, is not radio with pictures. Radio, the hot one, is not TV without pictures. Radio and TV are two very distinct media. The "hot" of radio and the "cool" of TV are examined in Chapter 11. The point here is that broadcasting is Janus-faced—the two faces, radio and TV, project very different personalities; thus each requires a unique emphasis.

The radio broadcast medium did not really mature until the camera came. Although radio listening has always been, innately, a very private, sitting-in-a-dark-room, person-to-person kind of experience, it was for a long time much misused as a family entertainment medium. This was caused by the pressure of the commercial imperative—the necessity (a command really) that radio make big money. Finally, the camera came and liberated radio by splitting the personality of broadcasting in two. Radio could leave to television the lighted face, retreat to the shadowed side, and become the very personal medium it had to grow up to be.

Even before the camera came, news broadcasting on the radio was already growing in this direction. I had my first lesson in person-to-person radio in 1945. As a very young broadcaster fresh from college and with a few years experience in local radio my dream came true. I was hired as a staff announcer by the prestigious WHAS in Louisville, Kentucky. At that time WHAS was a "basic" CBS station. This meant that a certain amount of network programming was originated by the station. In addition, WHAS was one of that now extinct species, a 50,000-watt clear-channel station—not another station on the same frequency in the whole United States! Watch out world, here I come! Since I had an interest in journalism, one of my assignments was to read the 11 o'clock (p.m.) news.

Never had my head been so large or my voice so booming. I had delivered about three of these newscasts on three successive nights in what I thought was flawless voice and style when I was unceremoniously called to the carpeted office of the chief announcing supervisor, Paul Clark. He was a tall, lean man who carried a big voice. He looked at me from behind large-rimmed glasses and said, "Wolverton, to *whom* do you think you are broadcasting?"

"Well, gee," I said, "I guess to just about the whole United States . . ."

"Uh huh, and all the ships at sea."

The lanky Mr. Clark took off his glasses and began to polish them vigorously. "What would you say," he said, "if I told you you had a total audience of *one?* One lonely little guy sitting out there in the dark somewhere, in his rocking chair, listening to his radio? Just you and him and the moonlight on the lake?"

I didn't say anything. I had never thought of radio that way before. I thought it was a *mass* medium. Millions were listening. But I didn't say what I thought. When Mr. Clark spoke, I listened. He returned his glasses to his face which magnified his eyes considerably.

"Radio," he continued, "speaks to each one of us alone. The ear is a very private organ. It is intolerant, closed, and exclusive. It winds in to the very soul of our person. Radio provides *privacy* for your man in the rocking chair out there, and immunity from his wife. He wants you to tell him in your own way, what's happening in the world, person-to-person. It's just you and him and the 11 o'clock news. Okay?"

So I climbed off my 50,000-watt clear-channel pedestal and I never forgot the old man in his rocking chair. He is still out there— he's the *only* one out there—whenever I read the news on the radio.

If you want to test the sightless nature of radio, and learn the difference between radio and TV, talk to a friend sometime in a totally dark room. Notice how the words of your friend take on new meanings and different textures. Without the lights you are blind and your friend's words give you comfort, even if you pay little attention to what is being said. When the lights come on, your friend's words are deflated—they lose much of their value. When the camera came to broadcasting, the lights came on. Television does not talk to you in the dark as does radio.

There are special techniques for the audio-only newscast. Its very private aspect is the basic one. If you work in radio today you work in a very personal medium. Each radio station has its own different and clearly-defined format. No other station in your market has identical music, news, or talk. If your station has top ratings it has a strong news department. News and information, interviews, and talk on radio have always been person-to-person. Marshall McLuhan, in his analysis of radio in *Understanding Media** writes:

> Radio affects most people intimately, person-to-person, offering a world of unspoken communication between writer-speaker and the listener. That is the immediate aspect of radio. A private experience.

It is a very private experience. My very first memory of this world is listening to the radio wearing a pair of earphones. Only *I* could hear! Today, my old man in his rocking chair has traded his cathedral-styled table-model radio set for a stereo headset with the radio (AM & FM) built in! Privacy. Complete immunity from his wife. The larger world shut out. At last a private world he selects for himself. It is the profound paradox of radio that to find the world we must first shut the world out. Only then can we become truly involved with others. This is a manifestation of radio's unique power to involve people.

It is not possible to become involved with the whole world as television lays it out for us, but it is inevitable that we become involved with one another on the community party-line that radio has grown up to be. And so the camera came to broadcasting and liberated radio from its slavery as an entertainment medium. Now radio is free to broadcast the news, the time of day, traffic information, and the weather. What all this means is that the radio newsman is different from the television newsman. It is difficult for us to remember this because we are all lumped together and called, "electronic journalists," or "the electronic press." But it is not so. We are not one lump—we are two. Of course we can and should

Understanding Media: The Extensions of Man, Marshall McLuhan, McGraw-Hill Book Company, ©1965, p. 299.

(but mostly don't) work together to stabilize our communities when they spin and flounder in the currents and whirlpools of national and international events. McLuhan has illustrated this when he discussed radio as the "hot" and television the "cool" medium*:

> We are certainly coming within conceivable range of a world automatically controlled to the point where we could say, "Six hours less radio in Indonesia next week or there will be a great falling off in literary attention." Or, "We can program twenty more hours of TV in South Africa next week to cool down the tribal temperature raised by radio last week." Whole cultures could now be programmed to keep their emotional climate stable in the same way that we have begun to know something about maintaining equilibrium in the commercial economies of the world.

The radio newsman must realize that he labors in a "hot" medium, one that *extends* a single sense and fills it with data. FM radio is "hotter" than AM radio because of its higher sound "definition" or fidelity. Either leave little for the audience sense of hearing to fill in, so there is little participation by the audience— little the audience can do to complete the message. It is this characteristic that compels involvement by the audience. Radio demands such complete involvement of the audience sense of hearing that all other senses are dimmed and a very private world is created.

Into this private world our news stories go. We will, therefore, select and treat our news stories accordingly. Because of radio's imperative to involve the individual, the native power of radio is its ability to involve people with one another in a *tribal* kind of way. And this is the power you wield as a radio newsperson. To be successful in radio news one must wield this power of involvement with authority. One must ask, "What items and techniques are the most involving?" As an example, weather is an item that involves almost all people equally, and, therefore, weather information should be at the top of our list of items to be broadcast on radio.

One of the most successful radio broadcasters was a regional network commentator and news broadcaster named Porter Randall. He always started his 7:30 a.m. newscast (on the Texas State Network) with the weather. It didn't matter what else was happening in the world, what was going on weatherwise across the great state of Texas came first. It has become a legend that when Neil

*Ibid.

Armstrong walked on the moon that July night in 1969, Porter Randall lead off his newscast the next morning with hail in Amarillo and flash floods in San Antonio! His second item began, laconically, "Last night, man walked on the moon ..."

Laugh—I did. But then on sober reflection I realized that this man, Mister Radio to two generations of Texans, understood and gave precedence to those items of news that had the greatest power to involve most of his listeners most of the time. You simply can't go wrong leading off a radio newscast with the weather, no matter what the weather is doing. You will involve your listeners immediately.

Traffic data is another item—accurate, up to the second traffic information—a hot item for radio broadcasting. Time signals, flashed frequently, even once or twice in a five-minute newscast keep listeners involved.

News bulletins, "This just in ... ," are highly involving. Don't miss them or try to decide if they are "worth" broadcasting. They are. Broadcast them the moment they arrive. Use a silent news printer and put it on the desk where you can read it while you are on the air. Interrupt yourself with, "This is just coming in over the wire, dateline Lower Slabovia ... " It will not matter where it is coming from or what it is. If it is a sudden breaking development it will involve your listeners because of its immediacy, not necessarily because of its contents. In this instance, at least, the medium is the message!

Other news items that keep the hot medium hot are stories with inherent human interest, or stories rewritten to point up the human interest angle. I once received what I considered to be the best compliment I could be paid as a radio broadcaster by another radio broadcaster. I was working for Gordon McLendon as senior editor for WNUS in Chicago, helping to pioneer all-news radio. In a memo to the news staff, McLendon wrote that my rewrite work on wire news copy was an example of what he wanted. His comment, in part, was, "... one of Mike's rewrites of a wire story on the death of a Chicago youngster sticks in my memory as a gem of drama and poignancy ... "

The drama and poignancy—the *human* interest—had *involved* one of my toughest critics. And since this was what I was after, this pleased me very much. It is easy to do. Figure out what involves *you* about a news story and write or rewrite with emphasis on your own involvement.

Another technique that is indispensible to the audio-only broadcaster is the actuality. Dialogue is hotter than monologue. Ask a question. Get an answer. And then broadcast it immediately. Use the telephone constantly. Get to the newsmakers and ask questions. Even a curt "no comment" is a comment with considerable involving power. Talk to some newsmaker in your community between each and every newscast. Tape, edit, and get it on the air as an actuality in dialogue. "A few moments ago we talked to . . . We asked . . ." Immediacy and dialogue are the hottest items in the hot medium of radio.

The most successful news programs I have ever done in radio have been the *live* studio interview with my community's newsmakers. You can't get more immediate than right now, so don't tape and playback later. Schedule the newsmakers right into your newscast or newsblock. I find that the noon hour is a very good time for this kind of radio news programming. The newsmaker can usually get away and come to your newsroom during the lunch hour, and most listeners are available because of their lunch break.

However you make contact with your newsmaker, via telephone, in person, or by going out with microphone and cassette recorder in hand, involve your listeners by involving yourself in the newsmaker's point of view. Don't succumb to the temptation to make your interview your own ego trip by trying to impress your audience or your newsmaker with your own point of view. Erase your own viewpoint off the tape and let your newsmaker impress you with his. Make it *his* ego trip. This way, instead of running the risk of making yourself the antagonist, you allow your newsmaker to cast that role. Ask questions about conflicts and how they are to be resolved. Let your newsmaker beat the drum that will pull *his* "tribe" together. That is what radio is all about.

Tribal Drums

A close tie-in with diverse community groups is the natural bias of radio. It summons the tribe and keeps it together. The tribe that listens together stays together! This is why ethnic radio stations have been so successful, both financially and in their ability to accomplish things within their communities.

All successful radio stations are "ethnic" in the sense that they program for a specific community. The rock station, country music station, easy-listening station, the classical music station—all program to summon a particular tribe. The radio station becomes the focal point for the tribal music, education, and social action.

The wedding of radio and phonograph has created a powerful new pattern of sound in the same way a singing group harmonizes its tones to create overtones—notes that are heard but that are not being sung.

The union of radio and teletype press creates no such power because the two do not harmonize. That note not sung is created only if the news is translated out of the teletype press idiom and into the colloquial speech of the tribe. When this is done, when the radio newsperson rewrites teletype press copy into the language of rock, or country, or black, or chicano, the tribe hears the overtones that carry the power for social action.

All radio news, editorials, and documentaries should be rewritten when broadcast to another "tribe."

Some of the radio news networks have tried to program newscasts for special or ethnic audiences by juggling content—by focusing on the special interest, or ethnic interest value of particular news stories. They miss the point. The news is the news is the news to all people. But different people resonate to a *way of speaking* that is indigenous to their group. It is not the black story that will speak to the black radio listener so much as it is a news story spoken in the words, phrases, inflections and syntax that are characteristic of the community of which the black listener is a part. The same is true of the country music listener, the rock listener, the classical music listener, or whoever the audience is.

Radio has the potential to unite the world and bring into being the Platonic political dream. That dream, however, must be broadcast separately to each private, small community, to each in its own tongue—for this soft, shadowed Janus-face of broadcasting allows us to share intimacies with the world at large in exclusive privacy.

11

What to Do When the Camera Comes

The lighted Janus face of broadcasting belongs to the cool medium of television. Marshall McLuhan says this about the principles of hot media and cold media*:

> The principle that distinguishes hot and cold media is perfectly embodied in the folk wisdom: "Men seldom make passes at girls who wear glasses." Glasses intensify the outward-going vision, and fill in the feminine image exceedingly, Marion the Librarian notwithstanding. Dark glasses on the other hand, create the inscrutable and inaccessible image that invites a great deal of participation and completion.

This principle is graphically illustrated by the women's liberation movement. If you study the images presented by women of the movement, you can formulate a theorem: *The more liberated the woman the bigger and clearer the glasses.* As women tried to "heat up" their image as persons they adopted king-sized granny glasses. Some members of the movement wear such large glasses that the feminine facial image is completely filled in, inviting little participation and effectively neutralizing the old image of sex object.

Much the same idea was applied to dress by the liberation movement. The woman with the huge glasses, attired in sweat shirt and

*Ibid.

blue jeans has filled in her feminine image so completely that, as a sex object, she demands little participation and completion by us. She now invites involvement as a person. She is now *person medium*—"hot," like radio.

On the other hand, those women who wish to remain sex objects will wear dark glasses. To paraphrase: Men often make passes at girls in dark glasses! The bikini serves the same purpose by showing the female form as sex object but hiding the erogenous zones to "create the inscrutable and inaccessible image that invites a great deal of participation and completion." Perhaps the addition of a bikini-type veil to cover the lips would make the "coolest" possible attire for woman as sex object! Sex, of course, is the coolest medium we have, demanding as it does the ultimate in participation and completion.

Television, then, is the woman in the bikini wearing dark glasses. Television is the sparsely sketched cartoon, like "Peanuts," that invites a great deal of participation and completion. The television image is one of low definition that must be filled in by the highly sensitive visual sense. The amount of visual information presented even by a color television picture is so far below the eye's ability to receive and process information that the "eye-sense" is compelled to participate and complete. The whole neuro-optical system tends to activate to fill in the data vacuum. In fact, television is so cool it tends to heighten the other senses and bring them into play. The sense of touch, so closely tied to the sense of sight, is especially activated. Television is not mute, of course, and does supply information to the ear. The sound of television is supplementary to the picture in a special way. It completes the sense participation and gives the viewer an experience in depth. That is why McLuhan defines television as:

> ... not so much a visual as a tactual-auditory medium that involves all of our senses in depth interplay ... a paradoxical feature of the "cool" TV medium (is that) it involves us in moving depth, but does not excite, agitate, or arouse. Presumably, this is a feature of all depth experience.

It is this essential coolness of the television medium that the TV news broadcaster must keep in mind and make use of as he goes about his task of gathering and reporting the news. He must keep his stories *cool* if he is to keep his audience participating in and completing his work.

I was privileged to preside at the birth of the 10 o'clock news on television. In the late 1940s in the twin cities of Minneapolis-St. Paul, Minnesota, KSTP-TV had signed on the air with a few hours of evening programming for some ten thousand TV sets thought to be in the area. I was at that time radio-TV director for an advertising agency that had added the "TV" to my title with the fond hope of enticing some of our clients to spend some money in TV. The gambit worked and the Twin Cities Chevrolet Dealers were coaxed into sponsoring the 10 o'clock news. My job was to produce it!

One would think I was well-qualified for the job. I had had experience in radio news and movie newsreels, and had spent a year trying to learn the ropes of television from Bill Colling, one of NBC's first TV directors. Also, I had written and directed a few TV dramas on my own, so the agency, the client, and the TV station considered me an "old pro." Apparently, only I knew what a novice I was! Those of us who pioneered the early flickering images of TV didn't know what we had. And we knew we didn't know. We knew that it was not radio, or the stage, or the movies.

"What *is* television?" was the question we asked ourselves over and over again, but like new parents with a new baby we had to let the child *teach us*. I gave the 10 o'clock news all I had to give and made all the mistakes in the book. Fortunately, for me, those were the days when people would watch anything anybody put on the air, including the test pattern, so the program was a commercial success, but not, from my point of view, a successful *news* program.

Reaction Cues Participation and Process Completion

Over the years, I did finally learn something about what television—and television news—was growing up to be. I learned two very important things: (1) television is a *re-action,* not an action medium, and (2) television is a medium that demands participation in *processes*. Television is more like a stained glass window than any other medium, with light coming through, not falling upon. It is much like iconography and could be thought of as an *animated* stained glass window.

The Mackworth head-camera, and other clinical devices, used to study how people watch television, proved the point about TV as a medium of reaction and participation. It showed that when folks watch television their eyes scarcely deviate from the faces of the actors, even during scenes of violence. It also showed that when we watch TV we watch for the reaction from those we identify with in order to be able to *participate* in this reaction. As television matured in the seventies, the most successful TV personalities were those "cool" reactors who invited participation by underplaying their roles—Mary Tyler Moore, Rhoda, Archie Bunker, and the coolest of all, Bob Newhart. The action that revolved around these TV characters was nothing much, but their reactions were something else again, so well understated that the audience had to complete the reaction. Walter Cronkite, considered to be the dean of TV news anchormen, was a reactor to, and participant in, the news of his day. We all watched him closely for those subtle clues he always gave us about how we should react to the news, whether it be a twinkle or tear in his eye.

In television news the audience is not a passive consumer of actions, as was the audience for movie newsreels. The TV news audience is a *participant in reactions*. From this principle the TV newsman has to take his cues about what to cover and how to cover it.

The state of the art has now progressed to the point where this can be done most effectively. The portable TV camera and taping equipment has freed us from the pitfalls of the movie camera. As long as we held a movie camera in our hands we were much inclined to "shoot movies." But with the new equipment, like the Akai units, we have in our hands a low definition, cool, TV camera. We are no longer making a movie, *we are now recording human experience in process*. Our most effective news stories will be those that present situations which consist of some process or action to be completed. Even if we are stuck with an old-fashioned movie camera to record our news stories for television, we must keep in mind that we are not filming high definition images that are highly involving for the eye, but low definition images as they will be seen on a TV tube. Images that will compel completion by the viewer.

In the early days of closed circuit TV, in the surgical rooms of medical training hospitals, students reported that they felt as if *they* were performing the operation instead of watching it on TV. Our TV news audience will feel as if they are participants in the events we record on our videotape recorders. We must look for themes of process and complex reaction. Television can illustrate the interplay of process and the growth of forms of all kinds as nothing else can.

In a TV documentary taped in São Paulo, Brazil, aired by CBS in the late summer of 1975 (on *Sixty Minutes*) we saw a city in process of growing almost beyond the limits of human endurance. This city was on its way to becoming the biggest city in the world, and in record time. Nothing could have illustrated the interplay of this process of *becoming*, like TV did. Nothing could have illustrated the growth of this grotesque form of human habitat as the cool TV tube illustrated it. No other medium could have invited more participation and completion on my part. Watching this process on television, I was there completing the form with my own greed and self-interest—contributing my own pollution to the general strangulation and suffocation of the human race. And having drawn me into participation in this grotesque process of growth my aching senses motivated me to more closely examine the growth of my own beloved city of Austin, Texas. Having *experienced,* I learned something about the dehumanizing influences within my own being and within my own environment.

Had I watched this same material on a movie screen in the splendid isolation of a darkened movie theater, it would have seemed a nightmare from which I would have desired waking relief. For the movie medium is a medium that takes us into a world that is like the world of our private dreams. And upon awaking from the dream, or, in the case of the movie, upon leaving the theater and walking out into the sunshine, I would have felt very thankful that it was only a dream or only a movie. My everyday waking world is nothing like *that!*

Had I read about São Paulo in the print medium, I would have been interested in the growth of São Paulo as information, but felt detached and uninvolved. I might have been compelled to act in some way, to give some money to the poor of São Paulo, but I would have done this in a rather disinterested way. The printed press imparts the power to act, without reacting.

Had I heard the material as a radio documentary I could very well have resonated to the tribal drums of São Paulo and felt impelled to join the migration in person! Indeed, they say it is the radio broadcasts penetrating into the jungles of Brazil that bring the natives into the city in hordes. Radio is the heart that pumps the life blood of cheap labor through the veins of free enterprise and keeps São Paulo's growth metabolized. They could, if they would, then, use television to "cool" and regulate this growth.

Television, then, differs from all other news media in its cool compulsion to participation and completion.

Tracking the Elusive Reaction

There is a second principle the television news broadcaster must keep in mind when taking cues about what to cover and how to cover it. Television, as we said, is a reaction not an action medium. To be effective we must go after the reaction story, and we must visually present the reaction element in any action story. To get participation in depth we let the *sound carry the action,* and we present the reaction to the viewer on the tube.

For example, take your typical city council meeting. A vote is being taken on a controversial issue. The issue has been heatedly discussed. All parties have been heard from. It is now time for the council to vote.

"Call the role, Ms. City Clerk," the mayor says. All eyes, including your television eye, are on the council members, right? Wrong! Your "ear," your microphone, is focused on the clerk and council as the roll call vote is taken. But your eye, your TV camera, is on the folks whose lives and fortunes are going to be affected by the outcome of that vote. It is not the action, the vote, you want to tape for your TV news audience, but the reactions that the vote will elicit from the people on each side of the controversy. And the reactions should be recorded in order of intensity. Try to pick the side that is going to react the most as your first reaction shot.

When I say "react the most," I don't necessarily mean the most hysterically. Don't confuse hysteria with meaningful and far-reaching reaction. If the vote went in favor of the neighborhood group that just saved their kids' playground from the clutches of the high-density developer, the neighborhood mommies may show the most overt reaction by sticking out their tongues at the developer's attorney. The attorney will probably take it all in with a poker face. But behind that poker face may be the perfect reaction. His client may want that playground so much that he will react by engineering a recall election to "fire" the dissenting council members, or go over their heads with a city-wide referendum on the issue, or maybe take the issue to the county courthouse if he has a legal angle. Get to him quickly. Get his reaction. It may be the one you will want to cut to directly from the council vote, and tack the protruding tongues of the mommies on at the end of the story as a stinger.

Take your typical police beat story. Usually, by the time we get to the scene, the action is all over. But the reactions are still happening. Maybe it's a wreck on the highway. Not really a news story since wrecks on the highway happen all the time, but someone is there who is seeing a wreck for the first time and is reacting to it. There is where you will focus your story—on that something new in human experience.

To show the action, or what's left of it—a crumpled car or a crumpled body—is to show nothing new. To show an injured person being lifted into or out of an ambulance is to show nothing at all. You might as well have stayed home and taken the footage out of a stock library, or reused the footage from the last wreck. The Neilsen man will certainly get you for that! Remember the Mackworth head-camera. Your television audience will be looking for faces that show reaction—reaction they can identify with and participate in.

In other words, cool it. And keep your cool. That is the power and the glory of broadcasting the television news.

12

Shading the Picture

Television news, requiring as it does the reaction shot as the keystone of the picture sequence, demands that we revamp our editing techniques. Most of us learned our editing techniques from the movies, and most of us started out using movie film to record our news events for TV. So, naturally, we tended to persist in editing sequences that presented what we call "good pictoral continuity"—establishing shot (ES), transition or medium shot (MS), close-up of the action (CU), and reestablishing shot (RES), which is intended to serve as a transition to establish the next bit of action. We used reaction shots mostly as "cut aways" to cover missed action—a kind of incidental insert in the total pictoral sequence. But even the moviemakers, nowadays, have weaned themselves away from the classical sequence of ES, MS, CU, and RES with inserts as needed. The moviemakers have come to a better understanding of their medium.

Motion pictures, as mentioned earlier, take us into a world like the world of our private dreams. When we watch movies, we turn out the lights and "close our eyes" to every-day waking experiences and retire into a dream world. When we have finished, we "open our eyes" by switching on the lights and walk out into the waking world once again. We can accept, indeed we may expect, the pictoral continuity achieved by the film editor to approximate the discontinuous nature of events in our dreams. And, as in dreams, continuity is in the sequencing of nonverbal symbols—the order in which the stained glass windows are installed.

Television, on the other hand, is always a part of our waking world. What we see on television must be wide-awake and real to us, lest the station suffer the wrath of the Nielsen man. It must be something we can participate in on the lighted side of our lives. The popularity of sports, news, and talk shows on television tells us that we turn on television for "the real thing." (Why do you suppose that slogan sold so much Coca-Cola on television?) We expect our television to be far more literal than our movies. If someone drops off the edge of the movie screen we accept it. If someone drops off the edge of our TV tube we want to know what happened to him. Why does the TV host *always* say, "I'll be right back . . ." before his image dissolves away into a commercial? He is saying, "I'm real, I'm right here, I am not a figment of anybody's imagination."

The Return of the Silent Movie

Editing for television, then, is quite different from editing for the movies. The sooner we get film out of our television newsrooms the better. The less likely we will be to fall into the trap of "cutting film," as film is cut nowadays.

There was a time when movies were "cool"—the editing techniques used then are quite applicable to television today. Those were the very early days of silent film when pictures were of low definition and flickered out of hand-cranked projection machines. When D.W. Griffith invented the close-up he used it primarily as a reaction shot. The early silent film was a reaction medium. It elicited a great deal of participation on the part of the audience. They supplied their own sound with cheers, boos, animated conversation, foot stomping, and often public sobbing. A study of these early American silent movies (from about 1895 to 1925) can be most educational for today's TV news editor, and I heartily recommend such a study.

A study of the early silent newsreels can be most helpful also, especially footage shot by combat photographers during World War I. Newsreels shot by Ray Fernstrom for Paramount on the Western Front during World War I, and his documentary on our saturation bombing of Italy during World War II, *The Earthquakers,* contain lessons in recording "the real thing" that should be studied by all TV newsmen today. I was privileged to work with Ray. We made theater newsreels in the early fifties and I learned a tremendous amount from this experienced and gifted man.

Although Ray had spent more than thirty years working in the tinseled trivia of Hollywood, he was still a master of the reaction shot. We came up with what I thought was some fantastic footage, reaction footage, low key, shot mostly in ambient light. It was not effective in the newsreel movie theaters, but when the TV stations and networks picked it up it was tremendously successful. Ray had warned me that we were going back to the silent movie days for our cinematic techniques. That's when I began to study the old flicks to try to learn why their techniques were so successful on television, particularly in news and news-documentary footage.

It was easy to see why our news footage and documentaries failed in the theater. What the newsreel theaters wanted at that time were quick snips and snaps of things utterly unimportant. They wanted Harry Truman gazing sternly into the camera. They did not want the people's reaction to their president. Newsreel theaters catered to vast and speedy audiences that enjoyed to gad about the world in fifty minutes and see almost everything. As the great documentary film maker, John Grierson, once put it," . . . they avoid on the one hand the consideration of solid material, and escape, on the other, the solid consideration of any material." The newsreel theaters certainly did not want to wake up their audience, which may be why they perished.

It was not quite so easy to explain the success of our material on television. After several months of studying old silent movies alongside the few successful things that had been done on television up to that time, I came up with our winning combination—focusing on reaction material, editing technique, use of sound to carry action, and a "cool" approach to visual images. What this approach does can be described by paraphrasing Grierson—on the one hand we considered solid material, and, on the other hand, we captured the solid consideration of any material we had to deal with.

Our editing technique was the key, of course. Our establishing shots were always short and to the point. We always cut to reaction as quickly as possible, and then we explored our reactions in depth. When we recorded sound with the scene, the camera was most often pointed in some other direction than the source of the sound. When we dubbed in sound later, we used it to reinforce the action, or to lend continuity to the action. Sound effectively underscored, lent atmosphere, and sometimes even poetry to the rhythms and tempos, crescendos and diminuendos of people reacting.

Much editing was done in the camera, which is often the only choice when putting the news on film. It became obvious, from studying the footage, that the less editing one does at the cutting bench, the better—for television. Just keep recording the reaction scene!

The Truth-in-Reaction Principle

Another discovery I made while analyzing these films and TV material was that pictures of the reaction scene almost never lied! Now we all know how easy it is to make pictures lie with conventional film editing techniques. But when one uses the camera to explore reactions in depth, with a minimum of cutting, and with sound focused on the action, the truth of the scene—the integrity of the story—is somehow almost magically preserved!

This "truth in reaction" principle can be more easily comprehended if one considers even the simplest of situations. A small child wrestles his hand out of his mother's grip on a street corner. The child darts out into the street directly in front of an on-coming speeding automobile. There is the scream of tires on pavement, but the car cannot stop in time and hits the child.

If we are filming this scene it is almost instinctive to "stay with the action" and film the child being hit and the lifeless body left on the street. But if, instead, we stay with the child and the on-coming car only long enough to establish the situation and a few seconds before impact swing our camera around into the face of the mother frozen in fear at the curb and film *her reaction,* we will have related the truth of the incident. For the truth is that this was a personal tragedy of a high order. If we are recording sound, our microphone may stay with the action, but our camera must swing one hundred eighty degrees away from the action to the reaction to tell the story "like it is"—a mother's unbearable tragedy.

Of course, if this were an actual situation we would drop our camera, snatch the child and then film the mother and child reunited, the child held tightly in the mother's arms—again the reaction. We would have missed little of the "truth" of the story by failing to get the picture of our own heroic action.

Not only does the reaction shot at the heart of the picture sequence tell the true story of any incident, it also avoids the questions of ethics and taste inevitably raised by showing violent or grisly action.

An NBC television crew missed an opportunity to tell the true story of war—humanity dehumanized—in a now famous bit of footage shot in the streets of Hue during the Tet offensive of 1968, a critical phase of the Viet Nam War. Most of us remember the Pulitzer Prize winning photograph taken by AP photographer Eddie Adams, which appeared in all the newspapers and newsmagazines. It showed a South Vietnamese police chief, General Nguyen Ngoc Loan, executing a suspected Viet Cong officer (in plain clothes) with a single pistol shot to the head. The NBC television cameras stayed with the action all the way to the blood gushing from the head of the corpse as it fell to the ground. For good measure the cameraman took a close-up of that blood gushing from the head of what had been a man seconds ago. Apparently he could not tear himself away from the action!

It was this close-up that became controversial back at the NBC control room in New York when the film was being videotaped from a satellite circuit. The close-up was not shown to us as we watched the evening news while eating our dinner. But some of the NBC news staff thought the close-up should have been shown because Americans were getting a picture of the war that was too "sanitized." They felt that it was the duty of the producer to "rub our noses" in the violence and gore of the war.

Suppose the camera had moved in on the executor just before he fired the fatal shot. One can see in the AP still photograph the impassive look on the face of General Loan as he kills another human being. Suppose the camera had followed *him* as he walked away from this act as casually as one would walk away from having swatted a fly! Would this reaction footage not have told the truth about war? That war is the ultimate dehumanizer? And with regard to taste and ethics, the decision of televising blood spurting from heads would never have had to be faced.

It is not only in the reporting of violence that the "truth in reaction" principle applies. It applies to the handling of all news if our aim is to give the public a picture of reality on which to base the decision-making machinery of a democracy. Nowhere is it more important than in covering political news, and nowhere is the principle more blatantly violated.

Senator Henry Jackson, during one of his forays as a candidate for the Democratic presidential nomination, once rightly protested the use of a still photograph. The widely distributed picture had been taken by a UPI photographer during an impromptu speech

Senator Jackson made in the town of Winter Haven Park. It showed him standing on a bench, speaking, and the backs of only three persons in the foreground, one of which was a child on a bicycle. The cutline that went out with the picture did say that there were forty or fifty people on hand for the speech, but that statement was deleted by most editors of the newspapers and newsmagazines who ran the picture.

The photographer probably had the best of intentions. He focused his camera on the action, Senator Jackson speaking, and included the few people in the foreground as compositional elements to make a pleasing photograph. But the picture lied. It made Jackson look ridiculous, as if he went about the country making speeches to audiences of three. Had the photographer turned his camera around and photographed the reaction, the crowd of forty to fifty folks listening intently, with Senator Jackson as the compositional element in the foreground, I'm sure the Senator would not have objected. And the news readers would have had the "true" picture of the incident. Had it been covered for television, we could have made the same mistake by keeping the camera and recording microphone pointed at the action. But our truth in reaction principle would have dictated that we keep the camera on the Senator just long enough to establish who was speaking, then swing the camera around, *away* from the direction the microphone is pointing, and photograph the reaction to the Senator's words in the faces of the people.

The reaction shot is not the incidental shot in the sequence. It is not something we "pick up" to cover missed action or to keep from having "jump cuts" in our final edited version of the story. (There is nothing wrong with jump cuts in news footage—it's honest!) The reaction shot is the heart of the sequence when we are editing news footage for television presentation. Cut to the reaction as soon as possible and then explore your reactions in depth. When recording sound with the picture, let your microphone follow the action. When dubbing in sound let it reinforce the action and underscore the atmosphere.

Had the NBC news crew moved their microphone in to a "close up" of the sound of the dying Viet Cong's last few heart beats, while their camera was on the executor, holstering his pistol and walking impassively away, they could have added a depth of the macabre that would have chilled the fervor for war far more effectively than showing blood spurting in living color.

Action and Reaction in Sound

I have applied the techniques I learned for television news in my editing of sound-only footage for radio broadcast news. They apply to news broadcasting in a very general way. In covering a news story with sound only, however, your microphone becomes your camera. Establish the action in sound quickly, then cut to the reaction sounds and explore them in depth. You may introduce a second level of sound—at background level to reinforce or lend continuity to the action. This serves as a counterpoint for underscoring and atmosphere, and it works most effectively with a directional microphone. As you focus on your "on mike" reaction sounds, the action sounds automatically drop down to background level. Radio, however, can carry the brunt of more action than television. Radio, remember, is the "hot" medium in which listeners are already involved and will likely imagine and identify with the reaction whether presented to them directly or not.

Television, however, is the reaction medium; its audience is "cool," more detached, and constantly looking for reaction clues. The journalist who uses a television camera to probe reactions in depth is using the medium to the limits of its capability, and, thus, is giving the viewers that picture of reality they must have if they are to function effectively. The advent of light-weight, portable videotape recorders and cameras will increase the impact of electronic journalism by sharpening that picture of reality and bringing it into homes with unprecedented immediacy.

The ENG Revolution

On a day in May, 1974, a million or so of us sat down to dinner only to have it grow cold while we sat transfixed by color images on our TV screens of reporters ducking bullets and police diving under their patrol cars for cover, while a house in Los Angeles with the "captors" of Patty Hearst still inside went up in roaring flames. We watched the action live from an alley fifty yards away from the guns. A news crew from KNXT-TV had edged into that position in response to monitoring their police frequencies. They had been tipped that the Los Angeles Police Department had found the headquarters of the Symbionese Liberation Army. Within half an hour of the arrival of the KNXT-TV crew, fifty local stations were picking up and rebroadcasting their coverage. By dinner time the networks had joined the pool.

This "see it now" coverage of an explosive news event brought to my mind a cartoon commentary I once saw on the probable climax of our technological progress. The cartoon showed a futuristic kind of TV receiver. On its big screen was the image of a bomb dropping out of an orbiting space station and falling toward the earth. The cutline read, "And now, in three-dimensional living color we bring you the end of the world!"

It was Armageddon for the poor souls trapped inside that flaming house. It was also the beginning of the end of film-camera news coverage. The most important technological development in television news since the advent of fast color film, what has come to be called the news minicam, was being baptized that day in May by the KNXT-TV news crew. The minicam has revolutionized TV news from its dinosaur age of film processing to its humming bird age of ENG (electronic news gathering). By the summer of 1976, all three TV networks were using only one-man electronic units (minicams) to cover the national political conventions.

The so-called portable TV camera was in use as early as 1958, but at ninety pounds and requiring a crew of three it was still a dinosaur. When the weight slipped to eleven pounds by mid-1970, the one-man minicam was born and the revolution was on in spite of its then high cost. In the words of KPIX, San Francisco News Director Joe Russin, "What we're paying for is the ability to be live, late, and local." With a minicam a story can be taped directly by the camera for later use, or it can be fed via microwave to the studio for use live or videotaped there for editing.

As television news swung into the competitive arena of "live, late, and local," a glut of non-news programming inundated the unsuspecting public and threatened to obscure news value judgment. The fact that a minicam unit makes TV news coverage immediate, versatile, and speedy is no excuse for covering the rescue of a Siamese cat from a downtown tree (Detroit's WJBK-TV), or for interviewing a Taiwanese acrobat who does not speak any English (Washington's WRC-TV)! We don't have to wait for an Armageddon, but we cannot lose sight of news values just because nearly everything is now accessible for fast reporting.

The minicam demands a polishing of the craft of reporting. ENG allows for no filmed retakes—no time to edit and narrate a story. In front of the minicam we must be ready to ask a question only once and keep our cool as we ad-lib any situation into the homes of thousands of viewers. We must be ready to work without an anchorperson, with reporters switching directly to one another for stories. As television newscasts become shorter, with more of them scattered throughout the day when they occur, we have to be more innovative in our news gathering habits. We must get the facts quickly and be ready, at a moment's notice, to turn camera and microphone on those segments of action and reaction that will make the viewer truly an eyewitness to the news.

As the dinosaurs go, so go the cruder techniques of cave-man news hunting. The old narrative techniques of voice-over film, the "stand-up voicer," the anchorperson, the keying in of still pictures and artwork, and other technique artifacts of the filmed news gathering age are anachronistic rituals in the age of ENG. Let them go. What you are is what you want to look like to your viewer audience—no newsroom mannequin, but a reporter on the job of reporting a story. You will look and sound like you have done your homework. Ask questions until you understand the situation yourself, and then explain it to your viewers. Most of the question asking activity will probably be done before the eye of the minicam, so be sure your questions are pointed toward understanding. Your viewers will see you doing most of your work as a working journalist. And what does a working journalist do? Explain complicated issues. And if the journalist does not understand them, he/she cannot explain them. Everytime your viewers are left confused by your television report you will have failed to do your job—even if you were the first reporter to get it on the air.

The journalist who survives the ENG age will do so by his/her ability to explain—to provide with minicam and minimike a picture of reality on which fellow members of society can act. The bottom line of broadcast journalism has always been to report the news as it happens. Radio has been writing in that bottom line for years with its battery powered news gathering equipment. Local disaster coverage via radio has given broadcast journalism some of its finest hours. Television technology has now put the television newsperson at the scene as news happens and put it on home viewing screens either live or just moments later. As television becomes more and more "late, live, and local," community reaction time will be able to keep pace with action in the community.

Part V

Relating to all those others.

13

Talking in Pictures

There is no equation between words and pictures. The old saw about a picture being worth ten thousand words is simply not true. It is like saying one peach is worth a bushel of pears. Words are verbal symbols and pictures are nonverbal symbols and they are processed by separate hemispheres of the brain. Some people tend to be more verbal than other people and so the statement that one picture is worth so many thousand words simply means that the person uttering the statement has a preference for nonverbal symbols.

We are all nonverbal to begin with. To the infant a mobile hanging over his crib (a picture) is worth an infinite number of words because he has no words as yet. When he learns the word "mama" and discovers that by uttering it, the most important person in the world comes running, the word is worth ten thousand pictures.

In the western world our culture is largely verbal. That is because our educational systems emphasize "readin,' 'ritin,' and 'rithmetic," all involving verbal symbol processing by the left hemisphere of the brain. There is not much emphasis on drawing, dancing, and drumming, which are typical nonverbal skills mediated by the right hemisphere. Thus we largely limp along on half a brain.

Yet, we give lip service to the idea that talking in pictures is ten thousand times better than talking in words. Why? Because what most of us mean by pictures is an image that we can translate into words. If we look at a painting of a landscape and somebody says,

"What is it?" we can say, "It's a mountain," or "It's a lake." What we have is a *verbal* picture, which is really no picture at all.

So-called "Modern Art" presents us with true pictures. We tend to feel that we do not "understand" the kinds of pictures painted by a Klee or a Chagall. What we mean is we cannot verbalize the picture. Naturally. It is communicating to us in nonverbal symbols. If we look at it and try to process the symbols with our well-educated left hemisphere, it makes no sense. We must view it with the right side of the brain. What we get, mostly, then, is a feeling. And if a picture makes us just feel something, we tend to think we have not really *seen* anything at all.

One of the most sensational, yet under-reported, news story of the twentieth century is the discovery by two physicists at the Stanford Research Center in San Francisco, California, that human beings have a "sixth sense" through which information can be processed in the form of nonverbal symbols for what they call "distant viewing."* In a series of well-controlled experiments Puthoff and Targ showed that there is an information channel of low bit rate processed by the right hemisphere of the brain through which we receive impressions of size and shape, colors, even sounds and subjective impressions about activities going on at a distant location. How distant? Well, the Stanford experiment tested subjects over distances of a few meters to four thousand kilometers. It appeared that distance didn't matter.

NASA was one of the sponsors of the Stanford experiments, because this information channel appears to be one that is nearly instantaneous even at cosmic distances—one that will be of great value to space explorers. It is, however, a completely nonverbal channel. It requires considerable training for an individual to be able to verbalize accurately what he or she "sees" with this sixth sense. The Stanford subjects had great difficulty describing what they saw—the impressions they got—in words. They had no trouble drawing pictures of their target objects even though they had had no previous talent or instruction for drawing. A commercial artist, like Ingo Swan, will receive much information on this channel. This information can only be pictured, there are no words—at least not yet.

*See "A Perceptual Channel for Information Transfer Over Kilometer Distances," Harold E. Puthoff & Russell Targ: Proceedings of the IEEE, Vol. 64, No. 3, March 1976.

It is important that persons responsible for broadcast news be aware of this lack of an equation between words and pictures. Since we must deal in both words and pictures it is important for us to know how our culture uses these separate verbal and nonverbal symbols and how to best use these symbols ourselves so our audience gets the "picture."

One of the greatest authorities on our culture and its symbols is S.I. Hayakawa. Closing out the first chapter of his book, *Symbol, Status, and Personality,* Hayakawa tells us about words—verbal symbols—and what they stand for in our society.

Some individuals are admired for their "realism" because, as the saying goes, they "call a spade a spade." Suppose we were to raise the question "Why should anyone call it a spade?" The reply would obviously be, "Because that's what it is!" This reply appeals so strongly to the common sense of most people that they feel at this point discussion can be closed. I should like to ask the reader, however, to consider a point which may appear at first to him a mere quibble.

Here, let us say, is an implement for digging made of steel, with a wooden handle. Here, on the other hand, is a succession of sounds made with the tongue, lips, and vocal cords: "spade." If you want a digging implement of the kind we are talking about, you would ask for it by making the succession of sounds "spade" if you are addressing an English-speaking person. But suppose you were addressing a speaker of Dutch, French, Hungarian, Chinese, Tagalog? Would you not have to make completely different sounds? It is apparent, then, that the commonsense opinion of most people, "We call a spade a spade because that's what it is," is completely and utterly wrong. We call it a "spade" because we are English-speaking people conforming, in this instance, to majority usage in naming this particular object. The steel-and-iron digging implement is simply an object standing there against the garage door; "spade" is what we *call* it—"spade" is a *name*.

And here we come to another source of identification reactions—an unconscious assumption about language epitomized in the expression "a spade is a spade," or even more elegantly in the famous remark "Pigs are called pigs because they are such dirty animals." The assumption is that everything has a "right name" and that the "right name" names the "essence" of that which is named.

If this assumption is at work in our reaction patterns, we are likely to be given to premature and often extremely inappropriate responses.

We are likely to react to names as if they gave complete insight into the persons, things, or situations named . . .

To realize fully the difference between words and what they stand for is to be ready for differences as well as similarities in the world. This readiness is mandatory to scientific thinking, as well as to sane thinking. Korzybski's simple but powerful suggestion is to add "index numbers" to all terms, according to the formula: A_1 is not A_2; it can be translated as follows: cow_1 is not cow_2; cow_2 is not cow_3; $politician_1$ is not $politician_2$; ham and eggs (Plaza Hotel) are not ham and eggs (Smitty's Café); socialism (Russia) is not socialism (England); private enterprise (Joe's Shoe Repair Shop) is not private enterprise (A.T.&T.).

This device of "indexing" will not automatically make us wiser and better, but it's a start. When we talk or write, the habit of indexing our general terms will reduce our tendency to wild and wooly generalization. It will compel us to think before we speak—think in terms of concrete objects and events and situations, rather than in terms of verbal associations. When we read or listen, the habit of indexing will help us visualize more concretely, and therefore understand better, what is being said. And if nothing is being said except deceptive windbaggery, the habit of indexing may—at least part of the time—save us from snapping, like the pickerel, at phony minnows.*

The habit of indexing has seen me through many an otherwise unintelligible news conference. It has saved me many times from taking the bait of the propagandist and the self-serving cause-promoter. It has enabled me to pinpoint the windbaggery in many a politician's trial balloon and explode it exposing great volumes of hot air inside.

Our culture uses and misuses the verbal symbols we call our language in strange and wonderful ways. It is important to keep in mind that these symbols—like all symbols—are characterized by meaning. It is the real meaning of the symbol that the broadcast journalist has to be sensitive to. The key to this sensitivity is the formula: A_1 is not A_2. The use of this key, to unlock understanding of issues to be reported upon for yourself, and to then convey that understanding, will ensure that your audience "gets the picture" in

*Symbol, Status, and Personality, S.I. Hayakawa, Harcourt, Brace, and World, Inc., New York, ©1953, pp. 15-17.

terms of verbal symbols. We must educate ourselves to question continually what our verbal symbols mean, at the time they are used. As reporters on human experiences we need to be aware of the degree to which these symbols pull our reality out of shape, and try to compensate accordingly in our reports.

Since the right hemispheres of our brains are largely underdeveloped and uneducated, little use is made in the mass media of true picture communication. Many "modern" artists and some avant-garde motion picture producers are experimenting in this area. Occasionally the advertising people come up with something comprehensible to those of us who are functionally illiterate in the area of picture symbolism—the Schlitz Malt Liquor Bull commercial is an example. But even this effort seems doomed to gravitate back into the realm of verbal symbols since we hear these modern artists talk about their work in terms of "visual syntax," "grammar of form," and "language of vision."

It will take much more experimentation of the kind initiated by the Stanford Research Institute before we can begin to understand how we "get the picture" when we communicate on a true nonverbal level. It is possible that the pictures we send over our television channels can become simple focusing devices enabling the audience to get highly individualized information through their own distant viewing channels. Television is "cool" enough to trigger this sixth, or distant viewing, sense if we can learn from our scientists what state of mind is required. Perhaps a meditative state? If we view television news, live, and use the images as a kind of animated mandala in a meditative mental state, could we then get much more information about the event via our own distant viewing capability?

Until the results are in from this whole area of knowledge about our culture and its nonverbal symbols, we will have to be content with the assurance that almost everything in the arena of human experience is some kind of symbolic event, comprehensible to us if brought to the verbal level but when symbolized on the nonverbal level is seen only "through a glass darkly."

It may be that those of us working the lighted Janus face of broadcasting need to consider how to report the nonverbal component of human experience, along with our verbal reporting. Perhaps we need to do this by taping reaction scenes that can be edited into a kind of continuity of experiences rather than a continuity of action events. Our sound—our voice over or our newsmaker's voice over—would carry the verbal information. Would this technique, then, give our viewer-listener a clearer picture of the sane or insane realities of our world? Might the insane realities be shown to be some disorder of nonverbal symbolic communication amenable to cure?

14

Sources and Sorcerers

That venerable comedian, Jimmy Durante, had a running punch line that became a trademark—"Everybody wants to get into the act!" It has always seemed to me that Durante must have learned this line, originally, from some broadcast journalist going through the morning mail. Everybody *does* want to get into the news act. And, sooner or later, nearly everybody tries. Few make it, but even so more get into the act than should.

What "sources say . . ." often bears no resemblance to reality; "usually reliable sources" are often highly unreliable; "sources close to . . ." quite often miss by a mile; and "a reliable source who refused to be identified" is usually the most untrustworthy of all. It is not often that a journalist has access to a real "Deep Throat." It is more often a *sore* throat with a scalpel to grind. Still, sources must be found and used. They must be handled so that the true winnows away from the false. Today's broadcast news reporter must learn how to relate to the news sources so that the sources themselves disclose the picture of reality we are always after.

Handling news sources is best learned while working as an investigative reporter. One starts from ground zero and starts digging. Here is how.

You use the telephone as if it were going to be disconnected within the hour. Call every possible source you can think of to get leads on other possible sources. You have a cassette recorder with a recording pick-up coil attached to the telephone. Record everything. After the fortieth phone call you often need to know exactly what some source said back on call number twenty-nine. These bits and pieces of telephone conversation are parts of a jigsaw puzzle you are trying to put together. In addition, keep a book of accurate notes, and keep them as if someone were going to destroy your tapes. Include your speculations in the notebook and connect them with arrows and lines to bits of information that you dig up to support your speculations. Your notes may soon look like the floor plan for King Minos' labyrinth, but you *are* working your way through a maze. Having these notes will help.

Good notes will reassure you when you feel you have fallen into Alice's rabbit hole, and it seems that it's all a fairy tale and your sources are putting you on—or setting you up! The notes will also show you where you need documentation. You cannot support your story by pyramiding one unattributable source after another. And your notes will be invaluable when you finally sit down to write your story. They will save running through miles and miles of recording tape, hunting for something you know is there, but where?

There are certain techniques all investigative reporters use most of the time. Not the least of which is shameless trickery. A reluctant source can often be persuaded to confirm information you do not yet have, if you pretend that you do have the information. Would he care to confirm or deny . . .?

A journalist has to be an actor—different scenarios for different sources. You have to grub a lot, and you should be quick to connect one fact with another and quick to rewrite the script. Be prepared to cultivate people—maybe some you would not otherwise be caught dead with. Softened by your seeming concern and grateful for your faked understanding, they'll open up.

Just don't get carried away and think you are the world's greatest sorcerer—Merlin reincarnate! Never forget that the only reason your pressure tactics and trickery work is that basically most people do want to talk to reporters. If you are really intent and interested in the subject you are investigating, that interest will transmit itself to your sources. It has a hypnotic effect. You know yourself that if you are approached by someone who is intently interested in what you have to say, it is hard to resist telling them what you do have to say. I have found that nearly everybody, except psychopathic liars, wants to tell the truth. I have seldom been lied to. Often, I do not get all of the truth from a single source, but remember, different bits of the truth from different sources will usually add up to the whole truth.

The art and craft of interviewing, like all other arts and crafts, must be practiced to be learned. There are techniques to be learned for getting into the home or office of a subject over seemingly unyielding resistance, for handling a firm declaration that no more questions will be answered, and for staying where you are obviously not wanted.

The basic technique is to be completely nonthreatening to the source. Be persistent, don't give in or give up, but do it in the spirit of being determined to do your job and report accurately—not as harrassment. To a direct request to leave and never darken the source's door again you might say something like, "Okay, but if I leave now there is no way I can report this and be fair to you. I don't have enough information . . ."

Handle the declaration that there will be no more questions by changing the subject to one the source is willing to talk about and initiate a conversation. Then try to steer the conversation back into your area of interest. But try not to ask any *direct* question when you get back there.

The best door opener I have found is to introduce myself quickly and then say, "Where can we talk in private?" When you do get through the door take the time to express your concern for the source's troubles. Let him know you understand that he or she *unwittingly* got into the trouble. Be gentle, be low key, and follow the golden rule, or, as my grandmother used to say, "You catch more flys with honey than with vinegar."

Hard-nosed investigative reporting brings into focus an issue that is always in the background of a reporter's work. And that is the issue of ethics. Perhaps the best, and even the most ethical, reporting in recent times was done by Bob Woodward and Carl Bernstein of the *Washington Post* on the Watergate Scandal. Yet even these careful reporters, working on the most substantive story in the nation's history fell into some of the ethical traps that seem to have been set, by whatever gods may be, for the reporters of this world to fall into.

In their book, *All the President's Men,* they relate the following incident. They were after telephone data on one of their subjects under investigation; a Bernstein source with the telephone company made this statement: "If John Mitchell wanted your phone records, you'd be yelling 'invasion of privacy.' " Bernstein has said that this statement posed an ethical problem that he had never resolved in his own mind. Why, he asked himself, did he feel that as a reporter he was entitled to access to personal and financial records, yet knew such disclosures would outrage him if he were subject to a similar inquiry by investigators?

Perhaps the most serious breach of ethics occurred when they tried to get the Watergate grand jury members to break their oath of secrecy. In this breach the reporters accused themselves of having chosen expediency over principle.

These and other ethical breakdowns related by the reporters themselves seem to have inspired other reporters to a kind of self-imposed blindness about *how* they get their stories. But how one gets the story is as important as getting the story. One cannot break the law to uphold the law—an ethical point often forgotten, apparently by some of our most prestigious law enforcement agencies. And no reporter must hold himself ethically blameless in spite of dubious methods because he feels his cause to be so noble as to be "above the law," or above human decency. Sources can be dealt with in an entirely ethical manner and still inveigled to reveal the information necessary for a reporter to unravel the cloth of deceit.

One standard of proof that Woodward and Bernstein imposed upon themselves in the Watergate reporting, however, should be adopted by all of us—they had at least two sources for everything reported as fact. This will help ensure that your sources are not deceiving, fooling, or lying to you. This is something you cannot allow, especially if your sources are elected representatives of the people in a democracy, or those working for such representatives.

Operators and Their Operations

The reliability of your news sources will always be uppermost in the mind of your boss. He/she is the owner of the license from the Federal Communications Commission that gives you permission to dig up and to broadcast the news. This person is a business person trying to make a profit. He/she is supposed to make this profit by "Operating in the public interest, convenience, and necessity."

Most of the responsibility for keeping the boss honest in his/her pledge to the federal government belongs to the news broadcasters. The boss's sales department is concerned with the peddling of air time. The program department is concerned with playing the numbers game to give the sales department that neat sales tool called ratings. The engineering department battles to keep the electronic gear running within the law, and other departments take care of the nitty-gritty of the day-to-day operations. It is to the news department of any broadcasting station that the operator looks to keep the FCC reassured that the station is indeed serving the interests of the public while making the operator a profit. It is important, then, for news broadcasters to understand the boss and the boss's problems: financial, legal, and philosophical.

The boss's financial problems all stem from unsold air time. There is little of this air time devoted to television news that is not sold. Even with a sales department that could not sell beer on a troop ship, most TV station operators have folk standing in line to buy television news. TV news operations, expensive as they are, seldom cause their operators financial problems. Television news has created a seller's market. This is not so often the case with radio news, even though radio news is relatively inexpensive to produce. There is, however, no excuse for this situation. Radio news can, and should, turn a profit for the operator at any hour of the day or night in any market in the land. When it does not, one finds the news department staffed by news readers who do little more than rip and read the copy that flows in over the wire service teletype machine.

As a broadcast news consultant, I'm often asked to turn a radio news department from a liability to an asset. It is not too hard to do. I get the news readers on their feet, their ears off the police monitor, and send them into their communities to find out what the people out there are concerned about. I get them down to city hall, around to the county courthouse, and up to the state capitol to find out what their elected officials are thinking and doing about the concerns of the people in their community. Then I give them a weekend crash workshop in basic journalism so that they learn how to report all this newfound information. Suddenly, the radio station has *news* on the air—a very salable commodity. Suddenly, too, the wire copy that is ripped and read has more meaning because the ripper-reader knows what concerns his listeners and how his local governmental agencies tie in with the national and international news hammering out on the teletype machine.

So much for the boss's financial problems. His legal problems are something else again. Television and radio news broadcasters share most of the legal problems with their boss. Although the boss may have some legal problems that do not involve the news broadcasters directly, such as proof of performance of advertising commercials, collections of past due accounts, and providing a program log acceptable to the FCC, most of the boss's sleepless nights are caused by the prospect of legal troubles the news broadcasts can bring. The boss cannot do his/her own reporting—he/she cannot check out all of the reporters' facts. The boss has to trust the news broadcasters and he/she usually does not like to trust anybody. It is not that the boss fears the news department might land him/her in jail, although he/she may have to worry about some member of the news staff being jailed for contempt of court for failing to reveal sources. The fears stem mostly from thoughts of fines and license renewal problems brought on by an increasingly vigilant FCC.

At this writing, a broadcast operator's license is good for only three years. Broadcasters are lobbying to have this changed to five years and there is little doubt that legislation will soon pass in the Congress giving broadcast operators their five-year license period. One of the reasons that this will happen is that the FCC itself is in favor of granting licenses for the longer time period. Then FCC Chairman Richard Wiley, addressing the Associated Press broadcasters at their annual convention in 1976, said, "The present three-year license renewal period means the FCC staff must consider 2,700 applications a year. I would like to see the commission use its time getting at those broadcasters who are not good public trustees."

Even if the boss figures he/she is the perfect public trustee, he/she can't help but wonder if the FCC is going to agree—or wonder if the news broadcasters are doing something that might incur the wrath of the FCC. The Federal Communications Commission is, after all, a government agency and as such is responsive to public pressure. And public pressure from special interest groups can be a nightmare, no matter how sincerely we try to serve the public interest.

Take the so-called "equal employment opportunities" law, for example. Under pressure from black and brown minority groups, no broadcast station operator could offer true equal opportunity, i.e., hire the most qualified person available for the job and pay no attention to his race, religion, national origin, sex, etc. The operator *must* offer quite *unequal* employment opportunities if those better qualified are *not* black or brown. Race and national origin thus become the prime consideration when hiring a news person if the operator is to be considered to be fair!

Historically, of course, the so-called Fairness Doctrine was the greatest headache of all—and possibly one of the greatest threats ever made to the broadcast operator. Under this abortive attempt by the Congress to legislate fairness, the first amendment was severely dented. It had the effect of shutting off a good deal of public coverage and debate. Broadcast editors had to confer with their operators' attorneys before putting together a program format that would not result in a ruinously costly and time-consuming demand for equal time.

Pressure in the fairness and other areas will never cease for the broadcast station operator, of course, but to push so-called fairness legislation to its ultimate length will be to finally tell everybody what they *must* put on the air. And that would end the news broadcasting business as we know it.

Philosophically, the broadcast station operator must "walk the line" as the old country song goes, between many special interest groups who dictate whom to hire and what to have them report as news, and the news broadcasters, who are always tempted to engage in advocacy journalism—disguising opinion as news. From one side or another the operator's constitutional freedom of speech and profit-making enterprise are continually being threatened. There is, however, help for the operator and it has to do with how we, as news broadcasters, see ourselves in relation to that elusive value called "freedom."

15

Orbits High, Orbits Low

In spite of the fact that we who broadcast the news know that we are tied financially, legally, and philosophically to our station operators and their operations, we still tend to think of ourselves as free spirits. "Don't shackle us," we say, "give us our editorial freedom. Leave us alone—let us get out there and get the news, learn its significance, and then let us translate what we have learned to our audience so that they, too, will understand."

Then gravity sets in.

We find that we are not free spirits soaring off into the wild blue yonder, but orbiting entities soaring from apogee to perigee always held in place by the gravity (pun intended) of that solid body known as the cultural institution. In our case it is the institution of "the press." We may orbit high or we may orbit low but we are always in orbit—never actually soaring free of the gravitational pull of the institution that launched us.

In the early 1970s, when the highest officer in the United States tried his utmost to bring two soaring reporters crashing down in ruins, he was unable to do so because those reporters were not as footloose and fancy free as they appeared to be. They were held firmly in orbit by the invisible field of a publisher, Katherine Graham, who had the guts to stand behind her staff and a couple of editors who skillfully maneuvered their reporters' orbits beyond the fringes of a political atmosphere that would have burned the team of Woodward and Bernstein to a cinder had they dipped into it at the wrong angle or with the wrong velocity. These were critical maneuvers, which, had they gone wrong—or had the reporters been allowed to go wild—would have resulted in the destruction of the whole concept of a free press. Most of our reporting is not done under these extreme, critical conditions. But the investigation and reporting of the Watergate Scandal did give us the limiting case that proves our point.

The point is that even though we are free spirits, out to get the news, we have to learn how to interrelate with the rest of the news team. That interrelation involves three elements: (1) the element of respect for the institution of the press, which in our case is created and sustained by our radio and television broadcast station operators; (2) the element of direction from those editors and news directors who stand apart from the day-to-day developments just enough to maintain a protective perspective for the reporters soaring in their orbits; (3) the element of harmony, of working smoothly and cooperatively with other reporters, writers, engineers, and producers occupying the same orbits.

The elements of respect for the institution of the press can best be engendered by an explanation of the place of the press in our western culture today. That explanation has best been expressed by a famous newspaper man, Walter Lippmann, who wrote what has to be one of the best books ever written about journalism, *Public Opinion*. Writing in 1922, before radio and television news existed, Lippmann put it this way:

> . . . At its best the press is a servant and guardian of institutions; at its worst it is a means by which a few exploit social disorganization to their own ends. In the degree to which institutions fail to function, the unscrupulous journalist can fish in troubled waters, and the conscientious one must gamble with uncertainties.

Lippmann goes on to say that the press is no substitute for institutions. Then, as quoted earlier in this book, he says the press is like "the beam of a searchlight that moves restlessly about, bringing one episode and then another out of darkness into vision." But, Lippmann points out, "Men cannot do the work of the world by this light alone." He maintains that they cannot govern society by episodes, incidents, and eruptions. "It is only when they work by a steady light of their own," Lippmann concludes, "that the press, when it is turned upon them, reveals a situation intelligible enough for a popular decision."

Our respect for the institution of the press, which is the servant and the guardian of all our other institutions, tends to be eroded by this lack of a "steady light of their own" by men who try to govern our society. Working mostly in the darkness, these people involved in affairs of national and global importance, when exposed, tend to blame the spotlight that is the press for their troubles. They play upon our guilt at having exposed them and try to engender disrespect for our searchlight. They try to get to the source of the power that operates the searchlight, our station operators, to get our power cut off so that they can go on working in the dark. But our operators know that there is no such thing as a little freedom of the press or a lot of freedom of the press anymore than there is a way of being a little bit pregnant or a lot pregnant. There is no way to diminish the freedom of the press, to turn the light down, without destroying it completely. It is this stubbornness on the part of our station operators to continue to supply the power to light the searchlights that we come to respect. And it is through this respect that we relate to that element of our news team.

The element of taking direction can perhaps be illustrated by an episode that is on the other end of the spectrum from the Watergate reporting in that it had no known impact on maintaining freedom of the press. But it may help to show reporters in their orbits the need to learn to relate to the editors in the news control room.

I was working as editor-newscaster on the afternoon shift of a metropolitan radio station, compiling my hourly five-minute newscasts from the two major wire services, voice reports from a regional news network, and from reports phoned in by an outside reporter I shall call Bennet who cruised the city in a radio-equipped car.

Bennet was a hard working reporter who took his job seriously and always managed to phone in at least one story every hour. Many times when the news was slow, his stories would be the highlight of my newscast. On other days when fast-breaking hard news stories were coming across the wire service teletype machines, Bennet would get crowded out of my newscasts entirely. This would make Bennet furious.

One afternoon the news on the national and regional level was developing at a pace I could hardly keep up with. There were some possible local angles I wanted to develop and so I radioed instruction to Bennet to cruise out and get me some comment, some reaction from city officials. But Bennet was doing his own thing, which, that particular afternoon, was to be hot on the trail of several police officers who were hot on the trail of a murder suspect. Bennet radioed in a series of suspense filled, but wholly insignificant, reports on the police chase. It had nothing to do with what was going on in the rest of the world that day—the news stories that had people glued to their radios. I was breaking several special bulletins every hour. As a result, Bennet did not get a single story on a single newscast all afternoon.

When my shift was over and I dragged myself wearily out to the parking lot at seven p.m., Bennet was waiting for me. He was going to have it out with me, beat me up right then and there. (The cops never got their man, by the way.) After some considerable verbal sparring, fisticuffs were avoided and I got Bennet to accompany me to the nearest tavern where I bought him a beer. We talked until well past midnight. With the aid of a few cold ones I was able to get Bennet to see himself as a very important part of a news team, rather than as a freewheeling, roving reporter, detached from the rest of the world and the events taking place in that world. When there were some sixteen empty bottles of beer on the table he began to see that taking direction from an editor did not throttle his freedom to report what he thought was important but was, instead, a way of responding that would keep him within the orbit of events that needed to be reported to the public.

From that day on Bennet related smoothly to that element which requires response: to editors and news directors who stand apart enough to maintain a proper perspective on the hour-to-hour and day-to-day development of the news.

The third element, that of working with other members of the team occupying the same orbit, can best be illustrated by returning to our original metaphor.

When the Russian spaceship *Soyuz* linked up with the U.S. spaceship *Apollo* for the first time, the final maneuvers required the two ships to achieve precisely the same orbit and the ultimate in cooperation between the crew members of each spaceship. There were high ranking military officers on board each ship, high ranking military officers of countries whose political leaders consider each other as enemies. Yet, in those final moments of linkup, there was between members of two nations who were ideologically worlds apart, the kind of friendly cooperation that is rarely exhibited by mankind. It was a moment in history that should never be forgotten.

The orbiting members of the news team, whether two reporters working together, a reporter/cameraperson, a reporter/audioperson, or a whole group of anchorpersons, reporters, writers, producers, and technicians working on the same story, need to study as sacred scripture the lessons taught by our pioneer explorers of outer space. They and the space scientists who back them up, are teaching the human race what it means to work with other members of a team. All egos are put in a box. All differences are set aside. The success of the mission is all that matters to everyone.

In the case of the news team, the mission is to give the information required for self-governing decisions. The job is not to *make* the news, but to *uncover* the news. The trouble we of the press have is not at all unlike the troubles of representative government where people conceive of themselves as free spirits. To return to the words of Walter Lippmann in *Public Opinion:*

> . . . the troubles of the press, like the troubles of representative government . . . go back to a common source; to the failure of self-governing people to transcend their casual experience and their prejudice, by inventing, creating, and organizing a machinery of knowledge. It is because they are compelled to act without a reliable picture of the world, that governments, schools, newspapers, and churches make such small headway against the more obvious failings of democracy, against violent prejudice, apathy, preference for the curious trivial as against the dull important, and the hunger for sideshows and three legged calves. This is the primary defect of popular government, a defect inherent in its traditions, and all other defects can, I believe, be traced to this one.

If we can truly learn to interrelate with all the other elements of our news team—that machinery of knowledge which we have now invented and organized and call the broadcast news—and interrelate in a way that will give our fellow citizens a reliable picture of the world, then our troubles and the troubles of government will fade away. The trivia that is now television and radio will also fade away and programmers will no longer be able to rationalize their trivia as "the hunger for side-shows and three-legged calves."

The other side of the coin of freedom is responsibility. Hang on to that feeling of being a free spirit out to get and report the news. But as you soar from apogee to perigee, never forget that you are also firmly anchored in a field of "gravity" known as *the press*. Gravity affects all things in proportion to their mass. And as we of the press become more massive in our role as servants and guardians of all institutions, so must we assume a greater load of guardianship over our own institution. Our freedom is grounded there.

Part VI

"Come grow old along with me;
The best . . . is yet to be . . ."

16

A Community by Any Other Name

Most of us broadcast newspersons know that we are of the community of the press. That is the community depicted on the side of the coin marked "freedom." But what is the community on the other side of the coin to whom we are responsible—the side marked "responsibility?"

Failure to identify with a community to which we are responsible brings forth most of our failures in the business of broadcasting the news. We must "invent, create, and organize a machinery of knowledge" for a *particular community* within our society. We must then use our freedom of the press to serve that community responsibility.

Most of us have trouble being part of a community because we are ambitious and feel pressured by ourselves and our peers to be upwardly mobile. We begin our careers with a local station, perhaps in the community in which we grew up, as I did, but our goal is a position with a national network. On the way up we do not allow ourselves to identify too much with the community in which we happen to be living because we know we are going to be moving on as soon as we can coax opportunity to strike.

Finally, we make it. Instant status. National exposure. We are covering the top stories—the very top ones! Everyone treats us first class, which is also the way we travel.

But what community do we serve? The national community? Is there such a thing? And if so, is it a community capable of nourishing one's roots? Many of us who have gone that way think not.

Sure, it's like being asked to join the College of Cardinals when you get offered a job with a network. But, after all, the College of Cardinals can only elect a Pope. There is no way they can serve a parish. For lack of a parish to serve I turned in my cardinal's hat a good many years ago. More recently many of my colleagues have done the same, apparently for the same reasons.

Writing about broadcast newspersons in *TV Guide** magazine, Marlene Cimons tells about a number of top network newspersons and their reasons for going back to local station broadcast news work.

"I'd had ten very disruptive years and decided I just wanted to become more locally involved," Cimons quotes Neil Boggs, a former NBC news correspondent. Boggs, who covered the civil rights movement, the 1964 presidential campaign, and the trial of Jack Ruby for NBC, now covers the Arlington, Va., county board for a local station, WMAL. "Now, when I go out and cover the county board," Boggs says, "I'm reporting on something that involves me deeply too. The audience and I have a mutual interest in what's at stake."

Bill Kurtis, who left the West Coast bureau of CBS News to anchor for a local TV station in Chicago, is quoted as saying that he feels the same way. "At the local level, ok, you don't have the world," he says. "But you can stick to one thing, and you can follow through with it, and you can communicate problems to intelligent people who can solve them."

Kurtis tells of an investigative story he did on the quality of medical care in a Chicago inner-city hospital that resulted in an administrative hearing into hospital practices.

"A three-year-old boy had died in the emergency room," Kurtis said. "His mother saw me on television and called me up. She said she'd had to wait two-and-a-half hours before she saw a doctor. By then it was too late. Her son, who had the flu, had gone into convulsions and died. The hospital contradicted her story. But I found a witness who supported the mother. Without my story there would

---

*"Big Fish Invade Small Ponds" by Marlene Cimons, *TV Guide,* Triangle Publications, Vol. 24, No. 35, Aug. 28, 1976, #1222, p. 12.

have been no investigative hearing." (The Chicago Board of Health subsequently placed the hospital on probation and made them improve the quality of their emergency care.) Quoting Cimons, now:

> Kurtis also says it is important to be able to take a news story and give it more than a cursory, on-the-air treatment.
>
> "You're in and out of stories on the network in such a short time, you can't stay with them, or you've got to condense," says Kurtis, who covered the trials of Angela Davis, Charles Manson, and Juan Corona for CBS. "I remember that the Cronkite show didn't take a piece on the Angela Davis prosecution case for a month. I spent one month not getting on the air. Then, when the prosecution rested, they asked me to sum it up in a minute and a half."
>
> Bill Stout, a former CBS news correspondent now a reporter with KNXT in Los Angeles, says there is a quality of dehumanization in working for the network, something he has not found in the local news operation. "When something happens, you cover it, you write it and you go on the air with it," he says. "It's not something you put in a sack and send back east."

David Schoumacher decided to leave the network scene after twelve years in Washington as a correspondent for CBS and ABC. He is said to have decided to leave after perceiving a change in both the public's attitude toward national news, and in his own feelings about what he wanted to cover. He felt that what happened in Washington was no longer relevant to people, they were more interested in knowing about their schools and about tommorrow's weather.

Schoumacher relates an experience he had after becoming a local station TV anchorman.

> "I was standing on a corner downtown one night when this big utility truck pulled up. The driver leaned out the window and yelled, 'Hey Shoe-may-shur! You're doin' a nice job!' People used to recognize me when I was on the network but they never came up to me. Now they think of me as their friend. That man even pronounced my name right—and that's never happened before, either."*

Marlene Cimons concludes her survey of more than a half dozen network-television news people who switched to local communities

*Ibid.

by saying that all of them spoke of the special pleasure in becoming close to their viewers.

It is this closeness to your viewers or listeners that will enable you to work effectively and successfully. It is this closeness that tells you what community you are a part of. If you have no viewers or listeners who feel close to you then you have no community to serve. Then you are only functioning as half a newsperson. It is the sad destiny of network radio and TV news people that they cannot serve the community in which they live, nor can they serve the communities in which their listeners and viewers live. They only serve a fiction called demography.

Demography is the science of the statistics of populations. Demographic communities are illusionary communities. It is the community where each family has exactly two and one-half children. In this world of half-children, and point nine automobiles, they have no need of a picture of reality on which to base their decisions. They are illusions. But it is for such illusions that network programmers program and network news producers produce. It is the monopoly board on which the numbers game is played out, a game that serves the advertisers who pay for the production of the news. But it serves no community of real people.

At the local station level the numbers game is played primarily to attract national advertisers. The principal players are the station salesmen and the ad agency time buyers. They play with their demographic chess pieces over expensive lunches. At this level the game can be rigged. The newsperson can rig it.

Audience measurement at the local level is real. The survey folks talk to people, real ones. They do not talk to any half-children or write down that a family in your community is driving point nine automobiles. It is only when the demograph of your community merges with the statistics from other communities that the illusionary community comes into being. As a non-network newsperson, you are no longer concerned with these higher demographics—the esoteric numbers.

To rig the game you must get out into your community and make your own survey. Your questions, however, are quite different from the questions of the demographers. Your task is to find out what the members of your community are most concerned about. Is it the schools and the weather? As a member of this community yourself, what are you most concerned about? Talk to your friends and neighbors about the things that you are all concerned with.

Where is it that the pictures of reality in your community tend to cloud up? What is it that is most needed to be known about in your community?

Take the concerns of your community back to the newsroom with you and use them to sharpen your editorial judgment about what to broadcast as the news.

If your news broadcasts cover the concerns of the real people who make up your community, they will listen to what you have to say and will watch the news your cameras point out to them.

The numbers game will be rigged in your favor. Let them eat cake in the sales office!

You will know you have succeeded in inventing, assembling, and organizing a "machinery of knowledge" for your particular community when you are hailed by the driver of that garbage truck. "Hey Shoe-may-shur! You're doin' a nice job!"

17

How to Stay Sane Even Though a Journalist

Those who have made the step down from the ozone level of network newscasting often speak of sanity. Bill Stout has said, "It comes down to a choice between the glamour and one hundred Holiday Inns and a bit of sanity and love at home."

Bill Kurtis says that taking the local job saved his marriage. With the network he was out of town two hundred and fifty days out of the year.

Neil Boggs commented, "It's hard to be a companion, father and husband. I had days when I would go down to the NBC studio at nine a.m., expect to be home later that night for dinner, and by noon I'd be on a plane to somewhere else. I'd have to pick up clothes along the way. For a while I had the world's largest collection of blue shirts, all purchased en route."

My own descent from the rarified atmosphere of communityless broadcast news work was made for selfish reasons of personal sanity, also. However, I found that even in the thicker air of local station news broadcasting it is not all that easy to stay a newsperson and remain sane. While family relationships improve tremendously, the very nature of the broadcast news from the frame of reference of community involvement can make unreasonable demands that threaten one's grip on what is important in this life.

I think the one thing that has saved my sanity while working as a newsperson is something I learned many years ago from a little book called *Science and Sanity* by Alfred Korzybski, who is recognized as the father of semantics. It is a book I recommend everyone read before embarking upon the semantic quagmire that is broadcast journalism. What I learned from this book was a *scientific orientation* toward life.

In advocating the orientation of science, however, Korzybski is not saying that we should all study physics and math or chemistry and biology. There are many scientists who do not have the orientation of science. And there are people with no formal schooling who have used this orientation all their life. It is called scientific orientation because science is the only activity in which this orientation is institutionalized. It could just as easily be called a journalistic orientation had the journalists institutionalized it first. It is an orientation required of all journalists.

Korzybski equates sanity with the scientific orientation. He says the sane person is one who (1) is determined to find bases of agreement that allow for some degree of intellectual and emotional flexibility, (2) is willing to put statements to operational tests, and (3) has internalized the knowledge that there is always more to be learned about everything, and who is therefore capable of listening. Sanity, so defined, i.e., the scientific orientation, is what we must all try to bring to our jobs, or communities, and our families. Scientists use this orientation to make more and more accurate maps of the territories they call realities. Journalists can use this orientation to draw better and better pictures of realities on which their communities can make better and better decisions in their task of self government.

In order to acquire scientific orientation, this thing called sanity, one must practice Korzybski's three points daily. To keep oneself in this orientation also requires daily practice. Every day tackle some disagreement you have with someone and try to find some basis of agreement that allows a bit of flexibility on the intellectual and emotional levels. Every day try to put some statement you believe to be true to some kind of operational test. Find out if it is really true. Every day try to listen to someone, or read something that will increase your knowledge in an area where you feel you are already pretty knowledgeable. Practice these exercises in your reporting work and in your personal life.

Korzybski says that if our evaluative processes were not crippled by our built-in misevaluations, we would all function so well that we would be regarded as geniuses! That may be overstating the case, but we can all certainly be enormously more inventive if we can just get the bugs out of our systems.

The responsibility to remain sane, even though we are newspersons, is pretty "awe-full." Our society can tolerate some degree of insanity in its social, political, and economic institutions. We can even withstand the impact of an insane president every two hundred years or so. We have our constitutional checks and balances. But most of all we have a free press to keep our communications lines open. And that free press must be composed of society members who (to paraphrase Rudyard Kipling) keep their sanity even while everyone around them is losing theirs.

The reason is quite simple. We use communications as a means of survival. Even the biologists among us have come to this conclusion. We, in the broadcast news, have hold of the very tool man has evolved to ensure his survival.

The English anatomist, J. Z. Young, says that man may be viewed as the creature whose specific technique of survival has been the development of means of communication. In his book, *Doubt and Certainty in Science,* Young develops some ideas about communication and cooperation in humans that every broadcast journalist shoud be aware of. And Young sees the development of television news broadcasting evolving from the very first physical symbol of communication:

In no other animal is the habit of assembly quite so well developed as it is in man. The biological significance of the habit is that by it the brain associations necessary for communications are formed. Some of the earliest of these assemblies occurred at prominent hills of suitable shape, on and around which large numbers of people came together. One of the clearest pieces of evidence that we have about early social man is that he soon began to build large artificial hills. Objects almost as big as anything we build now were the product of some of the early agricultural communities, nearly 10,000 years ago. Such huge objects are found all over the world—an English example is Silbury Hill in Wiltshire.

I suggest that the value of building these objects was that they and their names were the signs by which men were trained to react to each other in such a way as to make society possible. At first, this must have been learned by all coming together at one place. Ritual feasting . . . (and other ceremonies) are occasions of training of the brains of the members of the community, so that they shall continue to react correctly, and hence *get a living by cooperation and communication*. (Italics mine.) Mankind has gone on assembling and building assembly places ever since. It is assuredly one of the features that the biologist should notice about him.

The hill is a very convenient symbol because it is easy to ensure that the association is quickly formed. Everyone can stand or sit on the symbol while the ceremonies are performed . . . But there are obvious disadvantages about large symbols too. If they are to act as signs for the whole of a big population it soon becomes hardly possible to get everyone on or in. You can, however, have a lot of rather smaller objects or temples, in place of the original natural holy mountain. Their construction may be reckoned as the first act of making tools of communication, the direct ancestor of television. . . .

Before the holy mountain developed into television, however, an intermediate communications medium evolved. Young points out that originally each temple had its own spirit. But for the device to serve as a means of association for large and scattered groups of population, the idea of speaking of a single god whose *spirit* was everywhere arose. Thus, the same spirit could reside in any number of temples anywhere. Young speaks of this development as a discovery of very great power. The peoples who first learned it, he says, produced one of the greatest of human advances. The discovery certainly foreshadowed the development of the broadcast medium, whose electromagnetic waves can reside in any number of receiving sets anywhere.

The ancient affection for a central meeting place—a holy mountain—is to some extent active in all of us today, especially in the young as they mature. It is almost as if we must live again through the stage of ritual on a holy hill. The outdoor music concerts of the latter decades of this century, from Woodstock to Willie Nelson's Fourth-of-July picnics, would seem to be a reenactment of the music, dancing and drug-taking that occurred on Silbury Hill 10,000 years ago. And it is in the reflection on these modern day rituals of assembly as a means of communication that we can see the inevitable limitations of this tribal method of communication and how it threatened our survival. While it develops a cohesive, cooperating "in-group" within which communication is easy and secure, it also establishes an "out-group" with which communication is difficult, if not downright impossible, and/or dangerous.

In other words, if the man you meet at the Great Temple of the One Spirit greets you with, "Allah is great," and if you can reply,

"Allah is indeed great," communication is ready to begin. But if you are greeted by, "Allah is great," and you reply, "Jesus saves," you are in trouble! Communication is now not very probable. This lack of ability to communicate leads to the insanities that then begin to plague our societies and threaten the very survival the system was evolved to secure—according, at least, to the Gospel of J. Z. Young. The insanity is obvious when an African who calls himself black is terrorized by an African who calls himself white, when a Near Easterner who calls himself Jew arms himself against a Near Easterner who calls himself Arab, and insanity of insanities, when an Irishman who calls himself Catholic sends his *children* to war against the Irishman who calls himself Protestant! And vice versa.

But the antidote to this social poison has evolved alongside and as we all gather in the temple of Television, inhabited by the common spirit, Electromagnetism, and stare at the glowing screen that is our altar, for the ritual of the Ten O'clock News, we can apply the curative in massive doses. That is, if we ourselves are not too heavily infected with the good guys/bad guys syndrome. We can give our audiences the news with a scientific orientation—the sanity as defined by Korzybski.

The fact that the scientific orientation will overcome is assured by its nature. It makes intercultural communication possible because it builds ease and safety of communications from the bottom up instead of from the top down. It says, in effect, "Don't believe what I say is true because we both believe Allah is great or that Jesus saves, but because you can perform the same experiment I performed and prove it for yourself!" This way we can agree first about obvious and trivial things before agreeing about more general things, like the name of the true god. Science builds for us a whole body of trivial things which can be tested by anybody, Jews, Arabs, Catholics, Protestants, blacks and whites, and used by them to agree on the great generalities, like the true nature of gravity.

I am not suggesting making a god of science. That would be a throwback to the semantic absurdity of the thine-and-mine-holy-hill-communications-stopper. I am suggesting that if we adopt the scientific orientation we will retain our sanity in our critical role in the survival of mankind. The scientific orientation dictates a profound sense of social responsibility. It requires us to become so responsible to all people of all nationalities and religions that we are unwilling to go beyond what anybody who can observe and test can confirm for himself. We hold in check our own personal preferences for monogamy over polygamy, for our own political system over another political system, our own culture over another culture, because these are large issues about which testable statements cannot yet be made. Adopting the scientific orientation can, above all, make us able to maintain the optimum conditions of communications with *everybody,* especially those with whom we have social, political, economic, and religious differences. To intrude personal preferences into our work as broadcast journalists would be to cut off our usefulness as communicators and thus to make us impotent players in the drama of human survival.

18

Futures File

The center of our lives is no longer a holy hill or a temple in a distant city. It is a box in our living room that projects images. In our ritual ceremonies we use these images as the occasions for training our brains so that we will continue to react correctly, and hence enhance our lives through cooperation and communication. Since we live such mobile lives we also have supplementary boxes in our cars that project the sounds used in our ritual ceremonies all around us. Quite literally our senses are being extended so that we may all assemble and continue to organize our brains for the kinds of communications necessary to our biological survival.

Those of us who are in the ceremonial survival drama need to look at some of our most probable future human experiences. For this is the raw material from which we will write the script. That future can only be discerned intuitively, as is done in science fiction writing. So I make no apologies for the fact that what I am writing now is purely and simply, science fiction. However, the appeal of science fiction is that it tends to be precognitive and frequently gives the reader a picture of reality as it will come to pass.

Those boxes in our living rooms, in our cars, on our bikes, and in our pockets will continue to grow smaller but will present to our senses increasingly more realistic images and sounds. The entertainment presented to us will become increasingly more "true to life," that is, more true to the kind of life we will be required to live. There will continue to be that lag between those who choose the programs (the masses) and those who generate the programs (journalists/programmers) but the lag will lessen. The true-to-life entertainment programs will tend to merge with life itself so that most of us will be absorbed by what is happening, by what is going on in the universe, by what we now call the news.

Interest in purely provincial events will continue to decline at a rapid rate as the constituents of our communities relate themselves more and more to the larger events being experienced by all mankind. This development of interest was foreshadowed by the meeting of Arab oilmen that put your neigborhood filling station operator out of business. More and more, what happens in the Middle East, in Africa and Asia, and in Washington, D.C. will determine what is news in your community.

As man moves out into space, lives in space cities that orbit the earth and on other planets, those little boxes we carry with us will grow smaller and smaller. Finally they will become cyborg-type appendages of our brains to aid us in viewing and hearing at any distance, in any time, in any reality. This will be direct and instantaneous processing of information by our own brains. We will not be dependent upon electromagnetic waves as carriers of information. Already, the electromagnetic wave is becoming obsolete as a means of information transfer—ask any space scientist who has to wait nineteen minutes to get his information back from Mars and forty minutes from Jupiter. To explore the rest of the galaxy with hardware using electromagnetic waves would be absurd. It would be, as one scientist put it, "The long since dead communicating with the as yet unborn." Our human brains are already organizing themselves to process information through these new nonphysical energy channels.

All this is coming about in the rather distant future. Perhaps as far away as the latter part of the twenty-first century. But there will be an interim development in our present modes of communication that will increase the demand for broadcast journalism skills exponentially. This development will see multiple channel broadcasting from satellites in synchronous orbit around the earth.

Those little boxes we keep in our homes and carry with us will soon be offering sight and sound images from many, many more of the eighty-three channels they can now tune to. The images and sounds will be continuous broadcasts of special areas of interest so that everybody can choose what he wishes to be aware of at any time he chooses. One channel will continuously bring the news from the nation's capitol, the issues before our representatives in government. Another will broadcast news of the concerns of the United Nations and their members around the world. A third will bring us nothing but sporting events and sports news. Like a news magazine gone electronic, we will be able to tune to news of national and international affairs, life-styles, business, books, science, medicine, art, education, the entertainment world, and ideas and opinions of great people and ordinary people. In addition, there will be many channels devoted to entertainment of all kinds, dealing with our social, political, and economic concerns. Instead of one channel bringing us a variety of entertainment in linear time, we will have many channels bringing us many special kinds of broadcasts simultaneously.

All the variety of news events you now read about once a week in your favorite news magazine will be broadcast live and in color, and sooner or later in three-dimensional holographs, on all eighty-three channels our present TV sets are designed to tune to. The signals will be received on our boxes direct from satellites in stationary orbit 22,000 miles above the earth. The satellites will be relaying broadcasts from thousands of stations on earth, from earth orbit and from the moon. You will be able to select whatever you are interested in and hear it in any language you prefer. This will be a kind of tunable Tower of Babel—the ultimate hill.

All that will come about in the not-so-distant future. Perhaps as soon as the first part of the twenty-first century.

Meanwhile, we are into that barely discernable interface between science fiction and science fact right now. New knowledge and new technology is springing up within and without our profession like fruit flies hatching in a banana farm. While our own technologists continually present us with more sophisticated microcomputers to handle our editing chores—"super time base correctors" and synchronizers to literally paint pictures we have already recorded, altering hue, contrast, or anything else—we must simultaneously report such news as the creation of new life forms in the laboratory and the search for life forms already created out among the stars.

In my own broadcast news work I find that I am always looking for ways to apply our new technology of news gathering to the problem of translating what our scientists are saying and doing into English. Most of our scientists have not spoken English for years. The jargon of the scientific journals creates a real language barrier between the scientist and his community. This can have disasterous effects on science and the community unless the activities of the scientist and technologist become comprehensible to the general public.

This is not a "popular science" approach to new gadgetry. Nor is it the cop-out route of joining the fashionable bewailers of the adverse effects the latest technology is having on the quality of our lives, discounting the benefits our scientists and technologists are producing. It is a necessary communicatory function because our scientists and technologists simply do not have the competence to answer the questions of public policy that they raise. This is not even in the area of their responsibility. Their quite narrow skills are quite correctly aimed at uncovering new knowledge and working out increasingly more efficient *means*—and not to making choices about what *ends* we will want to achieve. Scientists do share in the public responsibility along with the rest of us and most have a good conscience about this responsibility. But the public does not speak their language and they have forgotten how to speak to the public. We cannot expect them, we would not even want them, to answer the fundamental social, political, and economic questions they raise. These questions must be put to us and to our news audience for we are the deciders of our ultimate fate—at least we'd better be. All who vote must be able to enter into effective discussions of nuclear energy, DNA recombinant research and technology, information services, and all those other issues spawning in our orchard this season.

An effective examination of the broad implications of science and technology is not beyond the scope of the layman if we can learn to perform our journalistic function properly. But we had better begin to understand such things as the new heavy particles that have physics in an uproar, and the astrophysicists' mind boggling world of black holes and incredible forces that stretch the laws of physics. You can be certain that our ideas about reality are about to be shaken to their very Aristotelian roots.

For those of us who will be working broadcast journalists through these final mind-warping years of the twentieth century the implications carried in these items are profound. If we are to bring to our self-governing community constituents a picture of reality on which they can base their decisions, it will take our best scientific orientation and all of our courage, our knowing, and our caring.

Afterword

... AUGUST 26, 2001 ...

THIS BROADCAST JOURNALIST IS CELEBRATING HIS
79TH BIRTHDAY TODAY ON ONE OF THE SPACE OUTPOSTS
BY REPORTING ON THE PSYCHIC PROBE OF A CREW OF
DEEP SPACE COSMONAUTS. USING AN OSCILLATING WAVE
THROUGH TIME, THE COSMONAUTS ARE COMMUNICATING
WITH AN ANCIENT REALITY SITUATED ON THE FAR SIDE
OF THE GALAXY. THE ENCOUNTER IS PRODUCING A
HOLOGRAPHIC IMAGE AT THE INTERFACE OF OUR TWO
REALITIES. THIS USED TO BE CALLED A UFO BEFORE
SUCH THINGS WERE UNDERSTOOD. THIS REPORT CAN BE
VIEWED ON CHANNEL 83 OF YOUR LITTLE BOX, OR IF
YOU ARE INTO DDV {DIRECT DISTANCE VIEWING}
PUT THE RIGHT HEMISPHERE OF YOUR BRAIN INTO
ALPHA-THETA AT 7 HERTZ, DEEP MEDITATION.
MY NEUROTRANSDUCER COORDINATES ARE AVAILABLE
ON YOUR MIS {MICROCOMPUTER INFORMATION SYSTEM}.
AND NOW, FROM THE OTHER SIDE OF OUR GALAXY,
THE NEWS.....

Bibliography

Byerly, K.R. *Community Journalism.* New York: Chilton, 1961.

Dygert, James H. *The Investigative Journalist, Folk Hero of a New Era.* Englewood Cliffs, N.J.: Prentice-Hall, Inc., 1976.

Epstein, Edward Jay. *News from Nowhere.* New York: Random, 1973.

————. *Between Facts and Fiction, Problems of Journalism.* New York: Vantage Press, 1975.

Fang, Irving E. *TV News.* New York: Hastings Publishing Co., 1972.

Friendly, F.W. *Due to Circumstances Beyond Our Control.* New York: Random House, 1967.

————. *Good Guys, Bad Guys, and the First Amendment—Free Speech vs. Fairness in Broadcasting.* New York: Random House, 1976.

Foreign Policy Association, ed. *Toward the Year 2018.* New York: Cowles Education Corp., 1968.

Fromm, Erich. *The Forgotten Language.* New York: Holt, Rinehart, and Winston, 1951.

————. *The Art of Loving.* New York: Harper & Row, 1956.

Garst, Robert. *Headlines and Deadlines.* New York: Columbia University Press, 1961.

Golden, Hal. *Techniques of Working with the Working Press.* New York: Oceana, 1962.

Harris, Thomas A. *I'm OK, You're OK.* New York: Avon, 1969.

Hayakawa, S.I. *Language in Thought and Action.* rev. ed. New York: Harcourt, Brace, & Jovanovich, Inc., 1963.

————. *Symbols, Status and Personality.* New York: Harcourt, Brace, and World, Inc., 1953.

Hohenberg, J. *News Media.* New York: Holt and Rinehart, Inc., 1968.

————. *Pulitzer Prizes.* New York: Columbia University Press, 1974.

Jackson, Gregory. *Getting Into Broadcast Journalism*. New York: Hawthorne, 1974.

Johnson, M.L. *New Journalism*. Lawrence: Kansas University Press, 1971.

Kabse, Sidney. *Modern American Journalism*. University of Florida Press, 1969.

Lippmann, Walter. *Public Opinions*. New York: Free Press, 1922.

_____. *Preface to Morals*. New York: MacMillan, 1929.

_____. *Conversations with Walter Lippmann*. New York: Little, 1965.

McLuhan, Marshall. *Understanding Media*. New York: McGraw Hill, 1965.

_____. *Through the Vanishing Point*. New York: Harper and Row, 1968.

_____. *The Medium is the Message*. New York: Random House, 1967.

_____. *War and Peace in the Global Village*. New York: Bantam Press, 1968.

_____. *Culture is our Business*. New York: McGraw Hill, 1970.

_____. *From Cliché to Archetype*. New York: Viking Press, 1970.

Menninger, Karl. *Love Against Hate*. New York: Harcourt, Brace & Co., 1942.

Miles, Donald W. *Broadcast News Handbook*. Indianapolis: Howard W. Sams and Co., 1975.

Peter, Dr. Lawrence J. and Raymond Hill. *The Peter Principle*. New York: Bantam Books, 1969.

Palmer, F.R. *Semantics, A New Outline*. Cambridge: Syndies of Cambridge, 1976.

Sevareid, Eric. *Not So Wild a Dream*. New York: Alfred A. Knopf Co., 1946.

_____. *This is Eric Sevareid*. New York: McGraw Hill Book Co., 1964.

Siller, Robert C. *Radio and TV News Guide to Professional Radio and TV Newscasting*. Blue Ridge Summit, Pa.: Tab Books, 1972.

Skinner, B.F. *Verbal Behavior*. New York: Appleton, Century Crofts, Inc., 1957.

_____. *Science and Human Behavior*. New York: Macmillan Co., 1953.

_____. *Beyond Freedom and Dignity*. New York: Alfred A. Knopf, 1971.

Wiener, Norbert. *The Human Use of Human Beings*. Garden City, N.Y.: Doubleday Anchor Books, 1954.

Index

Peter's parry, 68
Physicists, 12
Premises, major & minor, 26
Press, community of, 116
    electronic, 74
    institution of, 113
Promotions in broadcasting, 66
Protagonist, 9, 10
Public Opinion, 18
PR (public relations) information, 52-54
Puthoff, Harold E., 97

R

Radio, medium, 73, 77
Randall, Porter, 75
Rape, 36
Raw material, 8
Reaction, 89-92
Reasoner, Harry, 60
Recombinant DNA research, 50
Recording angels, 4-5
Reports, 14-15
Research, 22
Responsibility, 11, 30
Rockefeller, Nelson, 49
Roles, 3
Ruby Trial, 40
Russin, Joe, 93

S

Salant, Richard, 35
São Paulo, Brazil, 83
Schneider, Harry, 3-4
Science, 9, 50, 130
Science and Sanity, 122
Science fiction, 51, 127
Scientific orientation, 122, 125-126
Semantic indexing, 98-99
Semantics, general, 11-14, 122-123
Semantic value, 15
Short story, 9
Sirhan Sirhan, 29
Sixty Minutes, 83

Social behavior, 29
Sound-only editing, 91
Soyuz spaceship, 112
Space, reporting on, 60
Speech, freedom of, 108
Stanford Research Center, 97
Stout, Bill, 118
Style, broadcast, 60-64
Syllogism, 26
Symbols, verbal & nonverbal, 96, 99-101
Synopsis, 24

T

Targ, Russell, 97
Teletype press, 78
Tet offensive, 90
Time-space matrix, 37
Truman, Harry, 88
Truth-in-reaction principle, 89
TV Guide Magazine, 117
TV newscasts, structuring of, 51

U-V-W-Y

UFO (unidentified flying object), 49, 131
Understanding Media, 74
UPI (United Press International), 90
Verbal symbols, 96, 99-101
Viet Nam war, 90
Visual material, 51
Waiting For Godot, 42
Washington Post, 104
Watergate, 51, 104, 109
Weather broadcasting, 75-76
WHAS, Louisville, Ky., 73
Wiley, Richard, 107
Winchell, Walter, 35
Wire services, 48
WNUS, Chicago, Ill., 48, 76
Women's liberation, 79-80
Woodward, Bob, 104, 109
Word magic, 14
Young, J.Z., 123-124